HOW I GOT HAPPY

The Messy Truth About Healing Past Trauma, Building Emotional Strength & Getting Happy Again

Information For All Readers

This text discusses important life events, psychological concepts and mental health issues. The work has been checked for accuracy and relevance by licensed health care professionals. However, you should remain aware that this text does not act as a substitute for therapy nor should you rely on the content of this book as your sole means of therapeutic relief. You are advised to seek the input of licensed mental health experts who can make a proper diagnosis having regard for your unique circumstances.

Copyright © 2023 by LearnWell Books.

All rights reserved. No part of this publication may be reproduced, distributed, or transmitted in any form or by any means, including photocopying, recording, or other electronic or mechanical methods, without the prior written permission of the publisher, except in the case of brief quotations embodied in critical reviews and certain other noncommercial uses permitted by copyright law.

References to historical events, real people, or real places are often fictitious. In such cases, the names, characters, and places are products of the author's imagination. We do this where it's important to protect the privacy of people, places, and things.

689 Burke Rd
Camberwell Victoria 3124
Australia

www.LearnWellBooks.com

We're led by God. Our business is also committed to supporting kids' charities. At the time of printing, we have donated well over $100,000 to enable mentoring services for underprivileged children. By choosing our books, you are helping children who desperately need it. Thank you.

**This is really important.
It's a sincere thank you.**

My name is Wayne, the founder of LearnWell.

My Dad put a book in my hands when I was 13. It was written by Zig Ziglar and it changed the course of my life. Since then, it's been books that have helped me get over breakups, learn how to be a good friend, study the lives of good people and books have been the source of my persistence through some pretty challenging times.

My purpose is now to return the favor. To create books that might be the turning point in the lives of people around the world, just like they've been for me. It's enough to almost bring me to tears to think of you holding this book, seeking information and wisdom from something that I've helped to create. I'm moved in a way that I can't fully explain.

We're a small and 'beyond-enthusiastic' team here at LearnWell. We're writers, editors, researchers, designers, formatters (oh ... and a bookkeeper!) who take your decision to learn with us incredibly seriously. We consider it a privilege to be part of your learning journey. Thank you for allowing us to join you.

If there's anything we did really well, anything we messed up, or anything AT ALL that we could do better, would you please write to us and tell us (like, right now!) We would love to hear from you!

readers@learnwellbooks.com

We're sending you our thanks, our love and our very best wishes.

Wayne
and the team at LearnWell Books.

WELCOME TO OUR COMMUNITY

"It's like a private online book club"

Imagine if you could actually meet and talk with other readers of this book and share your experiences.

Imagine if you could chat with the author or join them on a live Q&A!

Imagine getting access to the author's notes and other exclusive, unpublished material.

You can do all of that and a lot more in the LearnWell Online Community!!

→ Download your **Workbook**
→ Chat directly with the author!
→ Meet and feel supported by other readers and their experiences.
→ Access additional, exclusive content about this topic and others.
→ Join our live Author Q&A sessions online.
→ Learn faster, make lasting changes, and have 10 times more fun!

All of this is part of our commitment to creating the best learning resources in the world.

Scan the QR code to get FREE access
www.learnwellbooks.com/happy

AUTHOR

Rose Killian

Rose grew up on a dairy farm in the Garden Route of South Africa. Nature, horses, travel, and creativity are her passions. But her major contributions continue to be in mental health advocacy. Rose is committed to helping others to transition from lives gripped by the effect of grief and trauma to lives of joy, happiness, and freedom.

Rose has completed tertiary education programs in counseling and certificates in various modalities of healing including meditation, Reiki and more.

Rose's life is a true gift to the world. Those who cross her path are fortunate that she possesses the strength to have endured her own life's trauma and the courage to share her story.

*I held your gentle hands and smiled
at your beautiful face as I wrote.
I wrote every word for you.
Chloe, you're strong. You matter.*

CONTENTS

PART 1: How Did I Get Here?   **13**

    1   You Are Not Alone   14

    2   Be Honest. Are You OK?   29

    3   Yes, Feeling Better Is Possible   42

    4   Action Begins When There's A Reason   54

PART 2: What Can I Do Now?   **71**

    5   There Is Positivity In Negative Emotions   72

    6   The Magic In Your Mindset   92

    7   There's Hope When You Can Cope   112

    8   Move Your Mountains With Micro-Goals   131

PART 3: What To Do Forever   **143**

    9   The Truth About Therapy   144

    10   Trust The Process, You're A Work In Progress   156

    Conclusion   168

    References   170

YOUR WORKBOOK

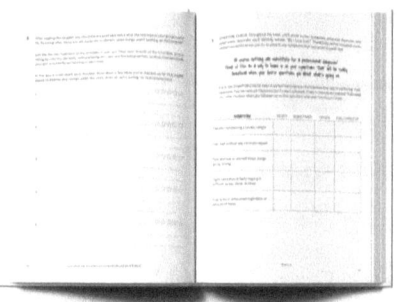

A shocking truth was discovered by a study done in 1987 – **people only remember 10% of what they read!**

That seems so discouraging.

But here's the **GOOD NEWS** – reading is **NEVER** a waste of time. As long as you do **one** important thing …

The same study (by National Training Laboratories) shows that you will remember 90% of what you read when you **put your new knowledge into action**!

Here at LearnWell, we aim to create **the world's best learning resources**. So, we have included a highly engaging **Workbook** that helps you put your new knowledge into fun, practical action.

So, make sure you download your **FREE Workbook.** You'll find it located inside the **LearnWell Community.** Simply scan the QR code below for access.

Get your Workbook in the LearnWell Community
Scan the QR Code for access or go to:
www.learnwellbooks.com/happy

INTRODUCTION

There are thousands of self-help books on the shelves selling the "answer" to all your problems. A common narrative is you just need to be positive and "look on the bright side of life." That's not what this book is about— healing is messy and takes work.

Although I have become an optimistic person, able to see the light in places I never could before, I'm not here to preach any toxic positivity or false hope to you. The hope you will find in this book is REAL. I know it's real because it's based on my truth; it's my story.

I sank to depths I never thought it was possible to rise from. I've dragged myself down, tooth and nail, wishing nothing but death for myself. But here I am, writing this book with so much self-love and acceptance in my heart that life feels beautiful again. The gratitude I feel for having a second chance at life and making it this far is enormous.

Today I write to you proud of my life and of my journey recovering from major depressive disorder, brief agoraphobia, generalized anxiety, panic disorder, severe self-harm, and bulimia. The victory was worth the fight, and all I could wish for is that this book encourages you to keep fighting until the battle is won for you too. It took me what feels like a lifetime to get here, but if I can share the tools I picked up along the way, maybe your journey can be just that much easier.

Loving you and accepting yourself in your full authentic nature does not mean you have never experienced pain. It means you have acquired the capacity and self-understanding to transform your view of yourself, others, and the world. It means you can face yourself with all your imperfections and divergence and embrace exactly who you are.

I'm not here to tell you to meet some one-size-fits-all standard. I'm here to assist you in discovering what your journey can look like and how you can recover and find joy again in a way that works for you. I've written this book to be as inclusive as possible in the hope it brings you, no matter who you are, the gold nugget of information you've needed to shift your life path in a direction that serves you.

I would feel every pain, go through every heartbreak, and relive every dark night I have lived just to fight my way out again and become the person who I am today. Although my life became filled with cracks and holes, each and every crevice is now filled with gold. Like a porcelain bowl put back together by the Japanese art of Kintsugi, I know my journey holds a beautiful story that needs to be shared.

Since my recovery, I have become a certified spiritual life coach and counselor with a passion for helping others find the light at the end of the tunnel. I want to see the spark reignite in the eyes of those struggling when they have an "Aha!" moment or see the dots of a bad situation finally connect. I know that feeling, and it's all I could wish for anyone reading this.

This life I live now and the person I've become was merely a distant dream smudged away behind the blurry lens through which I viewed life. Stability, self-love, and the joy in my heart were not always there. I had to work hard to fight my own mind while I grasped for solutions, struggling to see any glimmer of hope on the horizon. I had to slowly transform, like a butterfly curled up in its chrysalis, as my vision of life changed to the crystalline heart-shaped lens I look through today. I am able to let light flow into my life and transmute into a happiness I never knew existed.

So let me start this book by sharing with you how I got here, and then I'll ask you to take a leap of faith and trust me as we move through each chapter, one at a time.

You should also know that you won't be alone. The other readers in the LearnWell Community are with us. Run your thoughts by them at any time.

This book comprises 3 parts and a total of 10 chapters. Each section addresses a specific period along your wellness journey, and each chapter is vital to creating self-love and happiness in your life.

Part 1: How Did I Get Here? This section of the book is intended to jumpstart your healing journey. It's going to require you to dig deep and get honest. Don't worry; I'll remind you that you're not alone along the way as you put your best foot forward.

Part 2: What Can I Do Now? A toolbox of the most fundamental techniques and methods to get you feeling better as soon as possible. Don't skip Part 1 — you need to get real before you can heal!

Part 3: What Can I Do Forever? Helpful and healthy tips so you maintain positive progress for the long term.

I've written this book as a guide, offering you my story with the intention of sharing the hard lessons I've had to learn to get to where I am today. I know, because I've walked the walk, that the relief and progress you seek and need are attainable. My story is part of the light, it's a testament to change, and it's a hand extended to you so that you know we are going on this journey together.

 In each chapter, there are prompts that lead you to the Workbook exercises. Engaging in creative work will help to solidify your transformation. The exercises are guides to acceptance of yourself. And remember, read this book at your own pace and take your time with the exercises.

This is the chance to get your hands back on the wheel of your own life. Don't let this opportunity pass you by. Take it. You're worth it!

With love,

Rose

Please get your copy of this. It's really helpful

PART 1

How Did I Get Here?

1

What the caterpillar calls the end of the world, the master calls a butterfly

– Richard Bach

Fists curled, I wiped the sleep from my eyes, sat up under my Winnie-The-Pooh bedspread, yawned, and swiped my hair behind my ears. Something wasn't right.

The sun had already risen above the pine tree line outside my window, and sunbeams gleamed on the old wooden floor.

I slid my legs off the side of my bed and stood up with a loud *creak*. The wood was warm.

The cows were in their grazing field after their morning milking, and the chickens were dusting their feathers contentedly in the gravel driveway.

"Why did no one wake me up for school?" I thought.

I opened my bedroom door, and a personalized floral name plaque — 'Rebecca Rose' — was stuck to the outside of the door. I headed down the passageway past my older sister's room. Her poster-covered door, reading "Keep Out," was ajar, and the room was quiet.

Carrying on towards the stairs, a heavy feeling in my stomach weighed it down. I knew it wasn't hunger. This felt different in a bad way.

I grabbed the railing, walked past my three cats, Stoffels, Max, and Kitten — who all seemed a little frazzled — and when I reached the bottom, I turned the corner. My sister was curled up catatonic on the couch. Her eyes stared straight ahead. Instead of stopping, something told me to keep walking.

The night before had been a normal evening of homework, dinner, and bedtime stories with my mom. Nothing could have prepared me for what I was about to see.

There, sitting at the kitchen table with his head hanging in defeat, was my dad. He sat with shrunken shoulders, holding the pieces of my mom's favorite coffee mug in his rough, calloused hands. It was the first time I had seen my dad, my rock, with tears of despair in his faded beryl eyes. His heart was shattered.

My mother, the force that seemed to keep the cogs of our family unit turning, disappeared on a bus to start a new life for herself. She gave no warning, no explanation, and no goodbyes. She had made up her mind and, in a moment of impulsivity, was gone.

This moment, five months before my ninth birthday was the crux that set my life on a trajectory from which I, until recently, thought I would never return.

THE CHANGE

From that point on, my life became a whirlwind of confusion and pain. Unfortunately, despite every fierce effort my father mustered to keep our little family of three afloat, it was all too much for my developing mind to handle.

I blamed myself for my mother's disappearance. I wasn't an easy child and had so frequently been punished by her for my odd behavior and sensitivity. This is the only explanation that made any sense to me at the time, as my parents never fought, and no one had told me otherwise.

By my 13th birthday, self-harm had already become a secret crutch for me to cope. My appetite had become my enemy, and I felt throwing up every meal was the cure. My heart felt too small to hold the pain.

I had to teach myself how to "be a girl." Without my mother there, I was left to dwindle in the embarrassment of poor hygiene, messy clothes, and a lack of confidence to make female friends. I was bullied, excluded, and the subject of many jokes for being a "weirdo."

After a few years of progressive depression and severe anxiety, receiving nothing but a blind eye from the un-equipped adults in my life, the darkness that surrounded me became smothering. The ever-present gnawing that pained my stomach went numb. Ending my suffering possessed every thought in my mind.

My body was covered in hundreds of self-harm marks, ranging from fully healed scars to fresh cuts and scratches. Cutting made me feel alive. I hid the habit very well – not out of shame, but out of fear of what would happen if anyone found out. I evaded doctors, psychologists, or anyone that could help me for years.

Then, one night at 2:30 am, 6 hours before my final O-level geography exam, I turned the razor-blade in a new direction, down the length of my right arm, and began to take my life.

I fell into a trance-like state of tranquility, and everything around me faded into the background - every fiber of my being was consumed by the will to end it all. My heartbeat slowed, and I pushed harder on the blade until the gash was deep enough to be threatening.

At this moment, as the blade nicked the artery and the blood began to turn my bath water pink, a split second of sanity took hold, and I panicked. The blade hit the side of the bathtub with a clinking sound, and my heart palpitated as survival became its main focus.

The contrast from calm surrender to adrenaline kick made my head spin. I hurried to get out of the now lukewarm water. My arm throbbing in pain, I pinched my forearm around the elbow to try and stop the bleeding. Whispering, "No, no, no." I realized my mistake. I didn't want to die.

I continued to apply pressure while wrapping my arm in thick layers of gauze and medical tape. At this point, dressing wounds was second nature to me, but my confidence to secure this one was sinking.

After a few dizzy minutes of coming to terms with what I had just done, the bleeding slowed, and exhaustion took over my body. I did not wake anyone up. I did not call or message anyone. I just climbed into bed and went to sleep.

The next morning I wore a long sleeve shirt that barely covered the bandage. I managed to hide my transgression until after my geography exam — an exam that I wrote while haunted by the memories of what I had just done.

When I was finished, I handed in my paper with a smile, and my grandmother's tiny pumpkin yellow car pulled up outside the classroom. I hugged my small cluster of friends goodbye, and as I closed the car door behind me with a thud, I calmly asked my gran to take me to the hospital.

TRANSITIONS

Suicide is not always someone threatening to jump or writing an elaborate note. Sometimes it happens to unsuspecting teenage girls in the dead of night. It happens in secret and by accident. It happens and is a real endgame for untreated depression and misdiagnosis.

After this incident, I did receive professional help. I was sent to a GP that specialized in psychiatry, who put me on pills designed for fully developed adults. I was labeled with multiple diagnoses except for the one I so desperately needed.

My life continued to spiral in and out of major depression. I transitioned into young adulthood with a toxic relationship that only added to my trauma and confusion. The list of disorders and ailments kept growing until, one day, I suddenly snapped into what doctors labeled psychosis after another traumatic incident caused by my unhealthy circumstances.

I had gotten into smoking marijuana and found that it did, at first, ease my anxiety. However, once the side effects worsened, I decided to stop. I was already six months sober when I visited my mother-in-law for lunch. Janean was severely alcoholic and often behaved unexpectedly.

On this beautiful summer's day, my then-husband and I cycled to his mom's place. She had cooked up a lovely stir-fry with ample olive oil and fresh peppers from the garden. We ate willingly and enjoyed it. Everything seemed well.

After about thirty minutes, I felt a familiar nagging feeling in my chest. Waves of panic began to consume me. I excused myself to the bathroom and splashed cold water on my face. This usually helped me to snap out of it, but the feeling only intensified.

Starting to feel dizzy and nauseous, with my heart beginning to race, I kept my composure as I explained to my husband what was happening. Panic attacks were a regular occurrence for me, but I had learned to curb them. I hadn't had one in weeks.

Jenean offered to drive us home, and I was sure the attack would be over by the time we got there. Normally attacks peaked at 15 minutes, and I could "come down" to rest shortly after. But this time, the peak continued to climb.

By the time I got home, my vision had blurred. I kept trying to convince myself it was just a severe panic attack and that if I kept practicing all the techniques I had learned, it would subside. It didn't.

Falling to the ground before I could reach the front door, my heart felt like it was going to burst. The sky became a smeared blend of blues and whites. The solid ground beneath me morphed and swayed. "This is it." I thought as I mustered the voice to call out, "Take me to the hospital!"

Rushing through the double doors of the emergency room, my husband placed me on the hospital bed. The doctor hooked me up to a heart rate monitor and asked if I had taken Methamphetamine. I had not and could thankfully slur the word "No." My panicked expression pleaded with the doctor to do something.

As his eyes met the monitor and saw my rising bpm, he told everyone to leave the room and quickly closed the curtains around my bed. His change of tone and puzzled look made it clear this was something serious.

Before I could let that concern me, my eyes began to fade as I felt myself falling into a black abyss. They were open, but all I could see was darkness.

My body went numb as my mind became trapped in this void – I was certain it was death. Some part of me had always felt I wasn't meant to live long, so I surrendered.

Suddenly, a needle going into my left arm pulled me out for a second as my body convulsed with whatever drug the doctor had injected into it.

The void quickly swallowed me again, but I wasn't alone this time. Something told me I was going to be okay. It was like a familiar friend was with me, comforting me in this heavy moment.

One injection became two, then three as the darkness evaporated and the hospital lights stung my eyes.

The doctor sighed in relief, still holding the last syringe between his gloved fingers. My heart rate was stabilizing.

After he was sure the progress would continue and the beeps of the monitor steadied, he allowed my husband in to see me. Snickering, my husband walked in and confessed to the cause.

His mother had used a high concentration of homemade cannabis oil in the meal she had prepared for us. I had eaten the equivalent of at least 5-10 full doses in my stir-fry. The two of them found it hysterical. I did not.

From here, the word confusion doesn't even cut it anymore. This experience was my own personal hell, and the torment was not over. I did not leave the relationship for many reasons.

He was my high school sweetheart, so I didn't know any better, and I also relied on him for much of the little support I had in my life. Between my mom still living in another city, my dad struggling financially, and my deepening self-doubt, I stayed.

I was in and out of the hospital with severe blood sugar drops, and my daily life was plagued with intense panic attacks and traumatic flashbacks of the event. I was diagnosed with agoraphobia and panic disorder, then slipped into a mild psychosis.

Yet, it would still be years until I received an accurate diagnosis for my consistent struggle to function, both before and after the traumatic events that plagued my life.

Thankfully, this event was the catalyst for my long-term recovery. I finally landed in the capable hands of an experienced therapist who guided me to shore from the hellfires.

She helped me put a few pieces of my scattered puzzle together and slowly nurtured my introspection. This helped me understand that my current lifestyle and relationship were not sustainable. I understood that change was up to me, and I had a choice to make: life or death.

I started to live my life under a veil of discernment. I started to question everything and would not take no for an answer when it came to my well-being. I began researching and obsessing over the topic of happiness. And I started learning and applying lessons I will share with you in this book. I was not going to let myself sink to those depths ever again.

After a couple of years, my life looked very different. I had left the toxic marriage I was in, found love again, built up a career for myself, and started my path toward healing. But, I still struggled to maintain stability. Something still felt like it was missing, and my hope began to falter.

I was exhausted from trying so hard to keep up as an adult, fully responsible for myself but still largely unequipped to cope with my perplexing difficulties.

The familiar feeling of slipping away began to consume me again, so I scrambled to resist the downfall. I was not successful.

There I was again, struggling with my existence. It was impossible to shake the feelings of brokenness, fault, shame, or failure despite every moment of success I had earned. My foundation was crumbling beneath me.

With my hope a mere slither, I continued to deeply research topics in the line of mental health, psychology, and alternative healing. I needed to figure out what was wrong with me and what I could do to finally "crack the code."

I knew there must be something else going on that had been missed, or I was some factory reject the heavens forgot to throw aside.

I decided to give myself one last chance to redeem my belonging here on earth. I booked an appointment with a new psychiatric specialist in town for one last shot at a miracle.

THE RIGHT DIAGNOSIS

Purple fluffy pen in hand, I took out my favorite notebook, the one with the smooth pleather covering, and started writing. I wrote down a list of all the things I didn't understand about myself. I wrote down all my symptoms, all my confusing reactions to situations, and an in-depth background of my childhood.

At the appointment, my tired eyes gazed around the room as my anxiety forbade them to make contact with hers. I divulged every detail of my being to the specialist, which felt both overwhelming and comforting. I referred to my notes as needed.

Question after question, the assessment was a welcomed interrogation.

It was over. I headed to my car, my mind filled with the usual doubts, my notebook hanging by my side, my feet lagging. Was I simply overreacting? Was I perfectly "normal" and just a weakling? Maybe the struggle was all in my head. Isn't that where struggles lie?

And then, it happened. After weeks of waiting, my results arrived. The miracle I so deeply desired came, and I had that fabled moment where everything just "clicked." All the dots of my life, my trauma, and daily obstacles connected. The reality of my situation unfolded like an origami swan, intricate and detailed, with new truths revealed under every crease.

The diagnosis read Autism Spectrum Disorder with comorbid depression and anxiety, mostly due to growing up undiagnosed.

Regardless of what diagnoses I have received along my journey, getting an accurate diagnosis that tied everything together is what truly shifted my self-acceptance. Whatever journey you are on, know you are not alone. Even if you don't fully relate to my experiences, we are in this together. Mental struggles and deficits have many similarities and prejudices in society, and the information you will find in this book will hold value for you all the same.

Since then, the contrast in my life is what water is to a flame, from a nightmare of daily turmoil to the ebb and flow of sustained mental health. From one miracle to the next, it is my own personal marvel that I am where I am today - able to fully love and accept myself for all that I am.

THE JOURNEY

The journey has been arduous, and it is not one that ever ends. I know my life will never be perfect or typical, and I am okay with that. I have accumulated a well of lessons and knowledge that have helped me survive. I have learned to embrace and love every whisper of divergence that permeates me.

My path to deliverance was prolonged, and the delay almost cost me my life. It almost cost my dad a daughter, and my sibling a sister. And it almost cost the autistic community yet another undiagnosed member lost to suicide.

The desire closest to my ever-mending heart is that this story inspires you to trust your instincts when you know something doesn't feel right. Things never really felt right for me, even before the morning I woke up without my mom. I never felt like I belonged anywhere and often wondered whether I was even human at all.

Sometimes I think about the scars on my body and how many fewer there would be if I had simply opened up sooner and asked my dad if the depressive feelings I was having were normal. However, each one serves as a battle scar, reminding me of every mountain I have conquered.

Now that I've reached the point where I am confident enough to share my story with you, I wouldn't change a thing. I like to believe that everything happens for a reason and that every lesson I endured can help make your journey a little bit easier.

I know it can be confronting doing research to the extent I have. I know it can take a long time to find the right help to solve your problems. And I know it can feel easier to give up when you feel like the medical system has failed you. That is why I wrote this book.

Discerning what will or will not work for you is difficult with the boundless vats of conflicting information. I've been there. I've grasped out desperately for help in places I was assured I would find it. I didn't.

It took me decades to uncover the truths of my struggles. It took me pain, heartache, confusion, and failure. It didn't have to.

If I could go back in time and put this book in the hands of my younger self, maybe things would've happened differently. Maybe I'd have smiled in relief at the insights and learned to love myself sooner.

I don't want you to feel as lost as I have, searching blindly in a world that feels alien to you. I don't want you to feel helpless as you try the same old typical methods you've been told work for everybody else but somehow not you.

As hard as it is to believe sometimes, there truly are others who will understand what you are going through, no matter how isolated and alone you might feel. You don't have to reach the depths that I did to know you need to change your life.

And, if you know the depths I speak of and fear falling to them once again, I want to show you that you can climb so high above whatever struggles you are facing that your worries begin to shrink like ants in comparison to your strength.

I am going to show you what I've learned and guide you through an incredible transformation of self-care and self-love.

It's going to take courage, and I can't guarantee you overnight success. But I know that because you've picked up this book, you're ready to face this journey, and I'll be here with you to help lead the way through the dark.

 The most important thing you can do right now to start feeling better is to turn to your Workbook. Do the exercise provided for you, and I'll meet you back in Chapter 2, where we will start your healing journey by discussing the importance of acknowledging your pain in order to heal.

Let's do this together and leap into the unknown, trusting that you will be caught by the knowledge that's here waiting for you. The time to jump is now! I'm here with you.

2

BE HONEST.
ARE YOU OK?

*A man with outward courage dares to die;
a man with inner courage dares to live.*

– *Lao Tzu*

Without a word, my grandmother took me to the ER. She helped me out of the car with a subtle kindness and said, "Come now. Let's sort this out."

Long sleeves rolled up, bandages removed, I squeezed the edge of the hospital bed with my left hand while my right arm rested on my lap. The pain was crippling. Starting to taste the salt from my tears, I waited for the nurse.

As the nurse walked in, I noticed her emotionally charged expression. It was a look I was familiar with from childhood. I could tell she was about to yell — jaw clenched, eyes intense.

It didn't take long for the nurse to crack as her glare scanned my arms and took in the damage. "How could you do this to your parents?" She demanded. "What were you thinking? You're a selfish little brat."

The words hit me like broken glass, slicing away the last sliver of hope I had for receiving the compassion I so desperately needed. She roughly handled my wound, telling me I would have an ugly scar. Then she sent me home with the number for a doctor that could prescribe me medication.

I felt so misunderstood. The attempt wasn't about punishing my parents or being selfish. I didn't do it for attention or out of spite. Sitting with acute suicidal thoughts for months and not acting on them was excruciating. The fight to carry on was torture.

When you're caught in the clutches of severe depression or chronic anxiety, your brain does not function as it should. It can seem like the illness has a mind of its own. The behaviors and thoughts you exhibit might seem selfish to others. However, it is so important to take your feelings seriously, no matter what anyone else assumes.

THE IMPORTANCE OF AWARENESS

The weeks before I tried to take my life, my mind was overcome by disillusioned thoughts. I believed I was a burden to others.

The thought of removing myself from this world was not only to end my suffering but to end the suffering I perceived others were experiencing because of me. I fully believed no one loved me or would care if I was gone, not even my father. I believed the world would be better off without me. I was wrong.

The contrast between my perception back then compared to now is unimaginable. Since recovering and finding happiness within myself, I can see that the thoughts and feelings I was having were largely deluded by mental illness. I can acknowledge the unconditional love that my loved ones have for me and work through conflicts without seeing that love as faulted.

Depression and anxiety can hit you like a ton of bricks, or they can creep up so slowly that you look in the mirror one day and don't even recognize yourself. One morning I noticed the subtle shift as I woke up with the same unexpected sadness that I had fallen asleep with. Nothing that normally worked made it go away.

I tried watching my favorite movies, spending time outdoors with my animals, and working on a drawing I hadn't finished yet. At just 13 years old, I didn't know what was happening to me. Something had been feeling off for a while, but I didn't take much note of it until this point.

Every night I'd fall asleep hoping the rest would "reset" me like it used to. My eyes would open in the morning, and the sadness would persist. It loomed over me. My sister had mentioned something about depression she had learned at school and told me that's what I seem to have. I did not know what that would mean for me.

Then, before I knew it, as the years rolled on, the dark cloud became such a part of me that I didn't know myself without it. I quickly forgot what life had been like before.

Not understanding or fully acknowledging what was happening to me or the dangers involved, I learned to live with it. The weeks blended into months and then years. Ignoring my symptoms and trying to just get on with things — trying to fit in and be "normal" — led me down a path I almost did not return from.

My thoughts slowly twisted until I no longer cared whether I would get better or not. I embraced the cloud and started living life as the shadow of who I once was. The progression was slow and numbing. My eyes became blindfolded to the illness as I no longer rejected it. The familiarity of pain encompassed me. All the colors of my world faded to gray.

Depression is a dangerous game. The longer you play, the harder it is to return to safety. Once you lose yourself to it completely, bringing your true self back to life becomes an ongoing battle. Even the mildest depression is exhausting and can sow dangerous seeds of doubt in your mind that might later blossom into dangerous behaviors if ignored or left untreated.

This is why I urge you to start paying attention to how you are coping right now and admit the truth to yourself – no sugar-coating. This is the first step you must take toward healing and happiness. Awareness is the catalyst for your transformation. Don't pretend to be happy if you are not happy. You need to face who you are at this moment if you want to change your life.

THE TRUTH ABOUT DEPRESSION

Lying next to my sister after returning from the hospital, I could feel her tears soak my shirt as she sobbed against my back. My grandmother had dropped me back at home for the weekend. As cold and empty as my heart felt, this was the moment I realized how serious what I was going through was. Something shifted deep within me.

I realized that losing me would cause the pain I was so terrified to impose on my family. I realized that my dad and my sister sincerely loved and cared about me. It became clear that my struggles were affecting them because of their love for me. Like a flame, my sister's love allowed the ice coating my heart to slowly melt, and I started to acknowledge the pain I was feeling. It hurt, and for once, I didn't resist it.

Depression and anxiety can leave you empty and stuck as you grapple for relief. Like lighting a candle in a dark room, your acknowledgment can shed light on your struggles and help you find your way.

However, before you can see the light, you have to walk into that dark room, candle in hand, and be ready to face the shadows. You have to sit with your pain and recognize it. Take it seriously. It all starts with admitting to yourself that you're not doing okay. Then, you have to become aware of the things bringing you down one by one.

Although anxiety can become overwhelming, depression is the leading cause of suicidal thoughts and tendencies. If you aren't sure whether or not you are in danger of depression yet, or you aren't sure why you're depressed, I want you to consider this triangle:

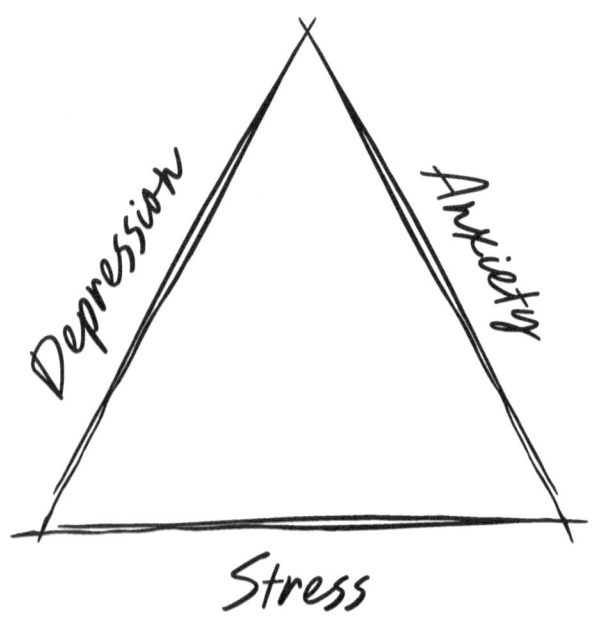

The diagram shows that anxiety, stress, and depression are linked. They are three sides of the same triangle, and you cannot have two of them without the other. If you are going through a stressful time in your life and have already developed anxiety, feelings of depression are likely to follow.

The same goes for if you are experiencing depression with anxiety, it is likely that there is some stressor in your life contributing to your suffering. Whether that stressor is a life event happening in the present, or a trauma that happened long ago, take it seriously.

Thanks to a recent "umbrella review" (2022)[1], conducted by Joanna Moncrieff of University College London, reviewing the last several decades of studies related to the relationship between serotonin abnormalities and depression, we now know that there is no convincing evidence that depression is caused by a chemical imbalance.

The study concluded that traumatic life events, aka environmental stress factors, are far more likely to cause an onset of depression. This goes strongly against the narrative many of us who have struggled with mental health have been fed: that the problem lies in brain chemistry and that serotonin-boosting antidepressant drugs are the cure.

Like the nurse shaming me for the cuts on my arms, it's easy to dismiss the cause when your focus is only on the symptoms. Sending me to a general practitioner rather than an experienced mental health expert only prolonged my recovery and made me feel fundamentally flawed and broken. Even though I wanted to get better in my heart, my symptoms and emotions were numbed with prescription medication, and I stayed sick and in the dark about why I couldn't shake the cloud that was following me around.

A CHOICE TO MAKE

Even if serotonin-boosting drugs could help aid in the recovery of depression, they would still <u>only be treating the symptoms of the illness and not the cause.</u> The boost would only be temporary without doing the active work to identify and heal your trauma and triggers.

A major traumatic event may cause anxiety, depression, PTSD, or a myriad of other mental health ailments that can be triggered throughout your life by minor causes such as smells, tastes, sounds, memories, and certain social interactions or experiences. These minor causes are generally referred to as "triggers."

Only once I started to identify the initial causes and subsequent triggers for my depression and anxiety could I start healing the symptoms and gradually feel better. This took a lot of courage and introspection as I revisited painful memories I had been pushing down. It wasn't easy, but it was worth it. The work I put into my own healing allowed me to experience the long-term relief of understanding why I was struggling. Let me say that again, the work I put into my own healing allowed me to experience the long-term relief of understanding why I was struggling. You have to rescue you; there's no other way around it.

Depression and anxiety are not random. There is almost always an underlying cause or core event provoking the onset of either one. Sadly the causes are not always obvious. That is why you have to dig deep and pay attention to the emotions and memories that stir inside you as you read this book.

Think about the pain you would feel if you broke a bone. Yes, at first, you might go to the doctor complaining about how much it hurts, but upon x-raying the area, you would notice the cracks beneath the surface. Mental struggle is much the same; only the cracks are the psychological wounds you have endured. Sadly, these wounds can be much harder to uncover as they don't leave physical scars. Yet, we can identify them through our posture, energy, and general disposition.

If you ignore a broken bone, the wound will fester, or the functionality of the limb will decline. Why would emotional wounds be any different? How can you expect it to heal if you do not acknowledge the wound and do the work to mend or support it?

Digging deeper and learning to identify what is causing you to struggle like this will open up the opportunities for healing you've been waiting for. Bear in mind that healing is not easy. It takes work, but it is always worth it.

Since recovering from mental illness, I can look back with a sigh of relief and thank myself for the bravery I was able to show in my darkest times. Without that bravery and determination to find the light, I would not be here where I am today: Happy and full of love for myself and the people in my life. I am proud of my younger self for standing up for her happiness and fighting for love no matter how much the darkness scared her. It hurt, and it was not easy, but it was worth it.

Whether you choose to do nothing and ignore your struggles or stand up and fight for your happiness, you will experience pain. The difference between the two is the long-term outcome for each. Both paths are difficult, but in the long term, one can kill you, and the other can heal you. So, just like I did, you need to choose life or death, love or fear.

Before you continue with this chapter, I want you to make this choice for yourself right now. Are you willing to do what it takes and face the truth behind why you are here reading this book? Are you going to choose love over fear?

I need you to trust me on this and start figuring out where things went wrong for you. Even though I am here to guide you, only YOU can turn your life around. Nobody else in the world can support or heal you as much as you can. I urge you to choose life, choose love, and give yourself the benefit of the doubt.

I have faith that you are ready and have the strength to acknowledge your pain. I'm banking on the fact that since you are reading this book, you are already on the path toward choosing life and love. Maybe you aren't sure of your choice yet, but just go with it and be open to where your journey takes you.

IDENTIFY YOUR CAUSE

Growing up diagnosed with depression, panic disorder, and generalized anxiety, I was made to feel like fear would be a part of my daily life for the rest of my life. With the help of my therapist and a lot of Journaling, I identified that the main cause for my early-onset depression was losing my mom and dealing with the stressors of adjusting to life without her.

It took a while for me to revisit this wound and acknowledge this pain point for myself. It wasn't easy, but it allowed me to start the healing process. I shone a light on the inner demons that told me it was my fault, and I managed to let go of the abandonment I felt. This took years, but the outcome was worth the journey.

I don't expect the wound to ever fully disappear, but I no longer fear it and instead embrace it as part of my journey. The wound resurfaces from time to time, and so do many others, but the more I am aware of it and its effect on me, the better I can work through it. The fear lessens over time when you face it rather than resist it.

I've also learned everyone suffers, and once we get on the other side of our pain, we engage with empathy, compassion, and love. I am here right now writing these words to help you, which is part of the positive impact of no longer being afraid of my pain. My wounds have ultimately become a catalyst for positive change and growth in my life, and I want to show you how you can transform and reconnect with yourself and others.

Being in the dark about my Autism kept me drowning in struggles without fully being able to recover as I waded in the depths of trying to live up to the expectations of my high-functioning, neurotypical peers. I couldn't help but compare myself to others and wonder how someone else could go through losing a parent like I did, yet not succumb to mental illness. Comparison is a scourge we need to avoid.

In this process of analyzing your life, both past and present, do not make this mistake. Don't compare your experiences or ability to cope with others and think you are not strong enough. If you are struggling more than you think you should, there is a reason. You just might not know it yet.

Go to your Workbook now and identify 6 core events that may be contributing to the struggles you are currently facing. Perhaps you've experienced a great loss, or maybe you're experiencing chronic stress of some kind. Think about what might be contributing to how you feel and write them in the space provided. This will allow you to get clear on *why* you are here right now and give you some peace of mind moving forward. You do not have to identify the moments, thoughts, or sensory stimuli that trigger you just yet; that will take time. Start by acknowledging the difficulties you have faced or are still facing that may have led to a mental health decline. Come back to me when you're done.

THE HARDEST PART

Now that you have identified the key things contributing to your unhappiness, doesn't it make a little more sense why you are struggling? Considering what you are dealing with, it's okay that you aren't feeling so good right now. You've done one of the hardest things you have to do on this journey by facing your pain points head-on. I'm so proud of you.

All you have to do now is keep going. Don't let yourself get stuck here too long. This isn't about wallowing in your pain but rather acknowledging that there are valid reasons for your struggles.

I know sitting with the memories and problems that are hurting you is one of the hardest things to do. It may even seem like moving on and feeling better is not possible.

I'm so glad I could prove myself wrong after believing I would never experience true happiness again. I forgot what happiness felt like and stopped believing it existed at all.

Now I don't believe that anyone is ever "too far gone" to start healing, no matter what you are going through or have been through. Depression and anxiety can suffocate your light so much that happiness and self-love feel out of reach. I promise you it is not.

You don't have to feel convinced of that yet, but you do have to be open to having your mind changed. Turn to Chapter 3 after completing the exercises in your Workbook. You'll soon catch a glimpse of all the powerful tools you will be given in this book.

3

YES, FEELING BETTER IS POSSIBLE

You, yourself, as much as anybody in the entire universe, deserve your love and affection.

– Buddha

The keloid scars that had formed on my arms were now dark purple. The weather was warm, and the sleeves of my school sweater were rolled up past my elbows. It had only been a couple of months since my suicide attempt, and I had just started at a new school. Everyone was staring.

Walking towards the field to have lunch on my own, a group of girls from the younger grades intercepted me.

"Did you get attacked by a tiger?" one girl said as she laughed wickedly with her friends.

Stunned with shock, I stood like a deer in the headlights as their cruel laughs echoed across the courtyard. I pulled the sleeves of my sweater down and tried to think of a comeback. Nothing. The question was silly but loaded with so much judgment it made the air feel thick.

The tears were starting to well up in my eyes, and my gaze dropped in defeat. But before the girls could say anything more, I heard a voice say, "Get lost, Abigail." It was a girl from my class, one of the "cool" girls, that sat in the back row with the boys.

She smiled and asked me if I was okay. I nodded and expected her to carry on walking. But instead, she invited me to sit with her group of friends. "My name's Jazz," she said as she turned to lead the way. Following behind her, my heart gleamed with relief. Maybe there was hope for me to fit in after all.

After what had happened the year before, having to face my family and friends following my suicide attempt, I lost touch with almost everyone and went into a quiet recovery. I did not want to leave the school I was in, but our car had already been repossessed, and I had to change schools to relieve the financial pressure my dad was under. Things had not gotten easier.

We arrived at the wooden deck where Jazz and her friends spent every lunch break. The group was made up of four rowdy boys, Jazz and another girl named Jamie. This was the rebellious crowd of my grade, but I felt right at home. To them, I was not an outcast. We were all misfits.

Jamie struggled with self-harm, too. Jazz had a broken home, and two of the boys came from families with addiction. None of them judged me for my scars or ever asked about them. I felt comfortable to be myself, but I was still barely functioning as a broken-down version of who I should have been. I was shy, quiet, and trying my best to just blend in.

One sunny day, my friends and I were all sitting on the wooden deck. The weaver birds were swooping around their nests, chattering loudly as they checked on their newborn hatchlings. It was early springtime and the beginning of our final semester.

We were talking about a party that had happened the weekend before. Noah was making everyone laugh, as he always did. He was confidently explaining what had happened after he had bumped into an old girlfriend at the party. Everyone was smiling and laughing and adding fuel to the fire with comments about what they had seen happen. It seemed like the perfect day.

Suddenly, time stood still as I took in the scene. Everyone was laughing and in a good mood, and I noticed myself laughing too. But deep down, I was only laughing because I knew I was supposed to. There was a silent emptiness within me, and I was disconnected from everyone.

I looked around the sports field in front of the deck and saw all the other groups going about their lunch breaks too. Some girls were leaning in, talking about the latest gossip. One group was having an argument. And another was playing with a ball on the pavement. But the thing that stood out to me most was how effortless everyone was living.

There were no signs of careful calculation behind their actions or anything forced. Everyone I could see was simply living out their lunch breaks on automation.

On the other hand, I was stuck in my head. My face was smiling, and I could hear myself laughing, but the emotions inside my heart were not matching up. All my behavior, down to my facial expressions and body language, was thought out in that moment to help me blend in with everyone else. Do you know what I'm talking about? It was like I was one step ahead of myself 'acting' my life.

Even this great group of friends that I was so comfortable with felt distant at this moment. I couldn't help but wonder, "Is everyone else faking happiness too?"

Despite all my efforts to be in recovery, all the medications I was taking, and all the good things I had going for myself, I still did not feel happy. It was clear to me that I was broken, or happiness just didn't exist, or at least that's what it seemed like.

Yes, there were a lot of changes happening in my life, but I was under the impression that I was coping with them well. It would not be the last time that I had this feeling either. However, there was one major reason why I was not seeing much improvement in my well-being. It had nothing to do with my circumstances.

TAKING OFF THE MASK

Before I was diagnosed with Autism, every social interaction I had felt like a movie scene where the other cast members knew the lines, and I had failed to receive the script at all. Conversations seemed effortless until it was my turn to talk.

Eventually, I built up my own set of lines and scripted behaviors to help me pass as normal. "Good, thanks, and you?" *Cue interested nods and a smile so they know you're listening.*

More often than not, I would cry on my way home out of sheer exhaustion and embarrassment as I analyzed every awkward silence and confused look. I was wearing a mask so tight that I had no clue who was underneath it anymore.

I knew I was suffering from depression and anxiety, and I was doing everything I thought I was supposed to do to get better. The only trouble was, without knowing the full truth about what was going on with me, I stayed in a perpetual cycle of Autistic burnout. I couldn't understand why I was not getting better.

With countless doctors turning me away with the same old information that was no longer helping me, I concluded that the problem was with me. I believed everyone else must be scripting and playing a role like I was and that I was not trying hard enough to succeed.

I stopped trying to recover and fell limp to the waves of anguish that had tried to wash me away all my life. I stayed sick for seven more years before getting diagnosed.

Since my diagnosis, I have had many revelations about why I had a tendency to fall into a deep depression at least once a year. I would fight like mad to keep it from consuming me, but nothing I did could keep the darkness at bay. Then, I figured it out.

All the work I had been doing to feel better and love myself was going to waste on this mask I was wearing. The mask was smothering my authenticity so much that I didn't even know the person I was trying to love underneath it. I didn't know who I was getting better for or why she even deserved to get better.

Since unmasking and meeting myself for the first time, I finally started my journey toward self-love and long-term recovery from mental illness. I went through a pivotal moment of understanding—you have to WANT to get better for recovery to last. However, you can't just want it out of desperation; <u>you have to want it out of self-love.</u>

That might seem like a riddle considering self-love feels like it's a million miles away in the throes of depression, but trust me, as long as you are alive, there is a light inside of you, and that is your self-love. Even if the flame doesn't seem lit right now, the wick is there, waiting for you to remember it and bring it back to life.

I know this because I was able to find self-love in the most unsuspecting places. I found it by forcing myself to do the things that I knew could bring me joy if I just let them. I found it when I started lifting the mask I was wearing and embracing myself in all my "weirdness." And I found it in the moments when I would look at myself in the mirror and smile to show myself what it would feel like.

Now, since growing this love within myself, laughter naturally comes, smiles are no longer forced, and I can do the things that bring me joy because I *feel* like it and not because I have to.

DEPRESSION IS A PARASITE

A very big consequence of struggling with depression for a long time is the inability to see that you deserve to feel better. The depression always told me that I deserved to feel bad. It told me I deserved to hurt myself and feel the pain when I cut my arms.

I didn't realize it at the time, as self-harm became a way for me to cope and find relief, but subconsciously I continued to do it because I didn't believe that I was worthy of anything better. Even when I was "clean" of self-harm for years, I still couldn't beat the urge to do it until I worked on loving myself.

Years of climbing in the shower forcing myself not to pick up the blade transformed into a peace that I had never known once I learned to love myself for who I truly was. The anxiety of stepping under the water, knowing what I was about to do, became contrasted by the blissful enjoyment of feeling the water against my skin and welcoming the experience with no thought of hurting myself in mind. This was an act that used to bring me fear but is now a place where I find refuge as I blast my favorite music and enjoy the normalcy of what a shower should be.

Depression keeps you in a cycle of numbness that can stunt your self-love significantly. You need to know that numbness is your body's way of protecting you from the emotional pain you are consistently putting yourself through.

I mean to say that you put yourself through because that's what depression makes you do. It makes you ruminate over past traumas, insecurities, and painful circumstances until it's just too much to bear. This is how depression takes its hold. It turns you against the one person you will always have in this world, the one person you are supposed to love above anyone else: Yourself.

Depression and anxiety work against you to try to remind you of all the reasons why you aren't worthy of feeling better. It makes you think that you aren't worthy of your own love. That is why depression is so difficult to overcome. It works to blindfold you from the one thing that will make you start healing—self-love. Like a parasite, it keeps you believing the lies it has told you to make sure you don't recover. Because if you don't love yourself, you are not going to care about getting better. It's as simple as that.

THE MISSING LINK

Before we continue, I need to make something very clear to you. Getting better is possible. No matter who you are or what you've been through, you are not a broken human. I suffered for so long that I was convinced without a doubt in my mind that happiness did not exist.

I understand that when you have forgotten what joy feels like, and what used to be daylight turns to an ever-present night; it can feel foolish to believe in something you have no proof of. But just as a caterpillar enters its cocoon, trusting that it will emerge as a butterfly, I'm asking you to trust in my story and know that the light is there, even though you might not see it yet.

<u>It is vital that you believe getting better is possible for you.</u> Without accepting this truth, you won't be able to move forward in your healing. You will self-actualize the outcome into reality.

For example, if you begin your recovery and start making progress but secretly you don't trust that it will work, the minute something goes wrong, you will use it as reinforcement for your belief. Life is not about things going 'right.' Once you understand this, you will not be able to use the 'wrongs' as excuses, but rather you will see them as opportunities for growth and change.

At the same time, if you believe that getting better is possible for you and you trust in the process when something goes wrong, it is easier to move past it as you know it is part of the journey. And you will continue to make progress.

You don't need to *know*; you only need to <u>*believe*</u> that getting better is possible. Once you *believe* it means you want it, and once you want to get better, you can start working towards it. You can't truly want something if you've told yourself it doesn't exist. At the same time, you can't want to heal if you don't *believe* you are worthy of feeling better. Remember, you don't have to know;

you only have to believe. That belief, along with self-love, will create the desire to heal.

This book is filled with the necessary tools you need for a long-term recovery. But the knowledge that is here will only make sense if you embrace your healing journey and move forward with an open heart. All of the teachings you will find in the pages to come are possible for you. There is nothing complicated or scary about them.

Now is your chance to change the narrative for yourself and take the next step forward on your journey. Let go of doubt and delusion and open up your heart to what's possible. You've caught out the parasite of depression for what it is doing in your life by putting the spotlight on it. It no longer has power over you and cannot govern how you will live your life anymore. You are ready now to move forward in love and take back the life you rightfully deserve.

I like to see this step as a formula that will keep you making progress no matter how many times you fall off track. This formula works by putting you behind the driver's seat of your reality, even though it was temporarily hi-jacked by anxiety or depression. The formula looks like this:

$$\text{Belief + Self-Love + Knowledge = Progress}$$

The formula for making progress requires your belief and trust that your hard work and patience will pay off. It requires you to see the value and worth in yourself so you can love yourself enough to keep going. And it requires the know-how.

Belief

+

Self-Love

+

Knowledge

=

Progress

In the previous chapter, you addressed the key things causing you to struggle. Now, I'm asking you to believe that you can overcome them no matter what they are. I'm asking you to be open to the knowledge waiting for you beyond Part 1 of this book.

Learning to love yourself is a process, and it's not something I expect you to magically whip up before you turn the page. What I am asking is that you stay open to the fact that you are worthy of your own love. You have to do the work to build trust with yourself again, but for now, just know that it's possible.

 Go to your Workbook to view the activities waiting for you. When you are done, I'll meet you in Chapter 4.

ACTION BEGINS WHEN THERE'S A REASON

*Happiness is a how not a what.
A talent, not an object.*

– Herman Hesse

Standing in front of the bathroom mirror, I tried to ignore the look of disgust on my face as I brushed through my tattered hair. Half of its length had broken off during the weeks nearing my suicide attempt. It had quickly become thinned out and damaged from the malnourishment and stress I was putting my body through. I had also not brushed it in weeks.

My hair has always been a good indicator of my mental health. It easily grows long and thick when I am happy, as it is now writing this book. But as I looked at myself in the mirror, it was clear my mental health was fragile. My lack of self-esteem had me in tears as I refused to go to school in this state.

Stern and with a look of deep concern on her face, my grandmother took my hand and turned me towards her. She looked me in the eyes and did something I would never forget.

She said, "When you have a problem, you DO something about it."

I need to repeat that: When you have a problem, you DO something about it.

Then, she picked up her old 1980s home phone and dialed the local hair salon. She made me an appointment, and instead of taking me to school that day, she took me to get my hair sorted out. To her, it was one less problem that I would have to face.

Her words, along with her actions, are what made this moment so powerful for me. She took the opportunity to help me rectify the problem instead of just trying to comfort me or yell at me.

I learned a valuable lesson that day; you always have a choice when you are presented with struggles. You can wallow in your pain and feel sorry for yourself, or you can stand up and take action to solve the problem. Even if you don't know how yet, just choosing to find a solution counts.

Although the concept is simple, in moments of distress and turmoil, we often feel crippled and unmotivated to take action. But this is the final, most vital thing you have to understand before proceeding with Part 2 of this book. You have to understand that your recovery is going to lie in the action YOU take towards YOUR healing.

You can have all the information in the world and receive all the best therapy, but if you, yourself, do not take action in applying this knowledge and DO THE WORK, then you should know that your progress will dwindle.

As you learned in Chapter 2, only YOU can change your life. So now that you are at this point where you are ready to take the next step towards your healing, you need to be prepared to take action and put the methods I will show you to the test.

I know that you are ready because you have already gotten this far. If you were not willing to take action, you would not have chosen to read a book like this, nor would you be reading it right now.

You are further along on your journey than you think! Maybe you have found yourself in a deep hole and have realized you need a way out. Well, this book is the ladder spanning the distance; now you've got to do your part and climb.

DO SOMETHING, ANYTHING

Sitting in the salon chair, the lights hurt my eyes, and the sound of the hairdryers engrossed my focus as my anxiety began to rise. All I wanted to do was run out the door. Before I could give in to the panic, the hairdresser tied a black tarp around my neck and smiled at me through the mirror I was looking into. She had a purple streak in her hair and was comfortably chewing gum.

After slowly brushing out every knot and applying a deep conditioning treatment, she explained that a lot of my hair had broken off and that there wasn't much she could do. She trimmed the edges and told me it was up to me to keep my hair healthy from here on out.

I still was not happy with the results, but I tried my best to use clips and bows to help me embrace the change.

Although my confidence took a big knock that day, the experience stuck with me for years. So many days came when I cried, feeling lost and stuck. Then I would sit up, wipe my tears, and hear my gran's voice,

 "DO SOMETHING ABOUT IT!"

Even if the action were simply picking up a book or taking a couple of deep breaths, I would take a step, sometimes a leap, at that moment to change my life's trajectory for myself.

However small the action is, when you are feeling lost and overwhelmed, you have to take action at that moment. You don't need to know the solutions yet; just do something, anything, to break out of that moment of despair. As long as it is something that will not harm you, do it. This will allow you to keep moving forward and make progress no matter what.

Sure, the easier thing to do would be to wallow in your pain and become a victim of your struggles, but the truth is you always have a choice to take your power back.

I know taking action when you are in a depressive or anxious state might seem like the hardest thing to do. Sometimes you get caught in a state of numbness that makes even moving a muscle feel impossible. But there is one thing that will keep you moving forward no matter what – a reason to keep going.

Even though this moment with my gran taught me a valuable lesson of strength, depression, and anxiety were always stronger. I spent years fighting the urge to give up and found myself failing over and over again.

The day my ex-mother-in-law drugged my food with cannabis oil, landing me in the hospital, my life spun out of control. Depression and anxiety began winning the battle once again.

When I arrived home from the hospital that time, I didn't get out of bed for days. I stopped eating completely and quickly lost myself to the dark hole of depression again. I was so weak after the stress of almost losing my life that I couldn't fight back. I felt unsupported by my husband at the time as he stayed convinced that it "wasn't a big deal," taking any opportunity to tell the story and laugh about it with our friends.

Bed became my comfort zone, and I watched animated movies on repeat to keep me lulled from my anxiety. Agoraphobia (the fear of leaving home) and stomach ulcers caused by the oil made a recovery feel even more out of reach. I couldn't walk out the front door without having a panic attack, and I couldn't smell food without wanting to throw up. All my symptoms slowly got worse. I ended up in the hospital twice more after this from severe dehydration caused by starvation. I'm not writing this book as some distance clinician who has never walked the walk. I know how uncomfortable mental illness can be, and I know how to help.

Eventually, all I wanted to do was give up. I wanted my decline to speed up so that it would all be over and I could have peace. Nothing seemed important enough to get up and keep fighting. This was because something big was missing in my life: I had no obvious reason to fight.

FINDING MY REASON

I had been dealing with suicidal thoughts for so long that simply wanting to be alive wasn't enough of a motivation to keep going. I felt isolated and alienated from the people in my life, and the one person who was in my life daily, my husband at the time, was so unstable himself that I couldn't rely on him for the love and support that I needed. Fear became my go-to once again.

The only friend I was in constant contact with called me one day to tell me he didn't recognize me anymore. He told me I had become a ghost of who he used to know. This made me feel shaken as I had not realized how bad things had gotten. But I also had no idea how to start getting better again.

Then, one day, I was alone in the house, lying in my bed, and I heard a sound at my front gate. I was living in a small cottage on a farm with my husband and our two dogs at the time. Because I was alone, I felt concerned and got out of bed to see what was going on.

In a moment that felt like some cheesy fantasy movie, a wave of awe washed over me as I realized what was causing the noise. There, pawing at my gate, was a young chestnut stallion named Prince that had been brought to the farm earlier that week.

I'm sure the feeling that stirred within me when I saw him had something to do with the chestnut horse my mom had left behind when she abandoned ship. Sparky and I had formed a friendship that I had forgotten about until this moment. I would sit on a fallen log in the forest near my childhood house, and he would calmly graze around me, occasionally nuzzling my hair out of affection.

As quickly as I could, I walked past the sink overflowing with dirty dishes and opened the fridge. I grabbed one of the carrots my husband had bought during his last grocery haul.

Reaching the front door, which was already open, I stood looking at the stallion contemplating whether or not I was willing to walk outside, under the colossal blue sky, just to give this horse a carrot. Before I could resist, Prince gave me a look of endearment that I couldn't ignore. So I did it.

I took one step outside the door and quickly felt the light hit me like a shower of daggers. I brought my hand up to shade my face and tried not to notice my increasing heart rate. With a deep breath in, I looked up and met eyes with this majestic creature at my gate. I took another step.

Before I knew it, I was one step away from the gate, holding the carrot out for Prince. He pressed down on the carrot as he bit into it, snapping it in half with a "crack." I stood there taking in this unexpected moment after the repetitive pattern my life had been stuck in the weeks before. Bits of carrot spattered out the corners of his mouth, and with a loud sneeze, he covered me in a foamy carrot-infused gob. For the first time in a very long time, I laughed.

From that day onwards, every morning, I would wake up wondering where Prince was. I began forcing myself out of bed and slowly attempted to explore the farm a little bit further each day, trying to find him. Some days when he was closer, I would find him and spend as much time with him as I could before the anxiety consumed me. On other days when he was further away, I would give in and go back inside. But still, I would push myself to go out and find Prince almost every day. He became my reason for a while.

Having something positive to focus on, something or someone to care for outside myself, made me feel motivated to get up and fight my fears. It was instrumental. Even just the small successes of leaving the house and covering more and more distance every day slowly increased my confidence and helped me keep pushing forward.

I can't stress enough how important it is to have a reason to get up every morning, no matter how silly or small it may seem. And that reason often stands outside ourselves, at least until we love ourselves enough to value caring for us as much as our external "reason."

FACING STRUGGLES HEAD-ON

One day Prince and the other horses were in the furthest field from my house. My husband had come home after fighting with his mother and was clearly in a rage. He started shouting and arguing with me about something I couldn't remember. Crying and begging him to stop shouting only made him more angry, and he gripped his hands around my face.

Middle fingers and thumbs pressing hard into my cheeks, he pushed me up against the wall. Without any idea whether or not this would escalate into something worse, I dropped to the floor and held my knees tightly in the fetal position. Realizing the fear he had just struck within me, my husband left the room.

After cowering in the corner of our room for a few minutes, I took off out the door in search of Prince. Unable to find him in any of the places I was comfortable with and filled with confusion about my home life, I kept going.

With the familiar feeling of tears burning my eyes, now red and puffy, I reached the corner of the field the horses were in. I sat down and continued to cry. The anxiety was beyond overwhelming but it was still better than being inside my home at that moment.

Once Prince spotted me, he started galloping toward me at an alarming rate. Unsure of what to do, being inexperienced with horses at this point, I quickly stood up and lifted my arms into the air out of instinct. He came to a sudden halt and reared up in front of me. Then he calmly walked towards me and sniffed my face with his velvety muzzle. My tears had stopped, and my mind was suddenly 100% fixated on Prince.

This moment ignited a strength within me I didn't know I had. It taught me that when I push myself past my comfort zone and face my problems head-on, amazing things can happen. This was the beginning of my journey with horses – A journey that helped remind me of the confident, strong-willed person I truly am.

Soon after this, I took up horse riding and eventually ended up adopting my own horse. Although that is a very big part of my continued journey fighting for my mental health, it was my initial decision to take action that led me to make progress.

I could have stayed in bed and ignored the pawing at the gate. I could have let the fear stop me from taking that next step towards feeding Prince the carrot. I could have kept cowering next to the bed when I felt like the main person in my life whom I trusted to support me had hurt me in a way I never expected. And, when I saw Prince galloping towards me, I could have turned around and run. But I didn't. What might be judged as 'small' actions to another person were 'monumental' steps for me.

<u>Find your steps!</u> Try not to overthink them or compare them to somebody else. And don't worry about having it all figured out before you make a move. Just focus on that first step ahead of you, no matter how big or small, and take it.

Every opportunity I saw, I took action. Even after I felt like the sky would swallow me whole if I stood beneath it, I took action.

Instead of running in fear, I stood my ground and took action. And it all started with discovering what my reason for getting out of bed was—for me, it was a horse that needed my attention.

I was lucky enough to have my reason find me at that time, but the more I look back, the more I notice a consistent pattern – there was always at least one main reason that kept me fighting for survival. There was always one thing bringing me a sense of purpose and joy. We start to notice our patterns when we start to heal. We start to notice our strengths as we start to grow the love for ourselves. This introspection and understanding come with time.

Like unlocking a chest filled with sand hiding treasures beneath the surface, you must unlock the truths within yourself, both good and bad. Decipher what is sand and what is a treasure, and you will come to learn what works best for you.

Sometimes when you've hit rock bottom, simply wanting to be alive isn't a strong enough argument to keep going forward. It isn't easy to get out of bed every day and do the things you need to do to keep yourself healthy when you don't know why you're doing it. This is why it is so important to find a reason to get up every morning.

You need to have something you're willing to live for when you can't see the value in living for yourself alone. Your reason can change over time, but for now, just recognizing one thing that motivates you to get out of bed every morning is enough to change your life. This is the thing you need to focus on right now to keep pushing yourself forward and taking those monumental steps for yourself.

WHAT IS YOUR REASON?

Not everyone is going to have a somewhat mystical experience with an animal that helps bring them out of a dark place. But no matter how down and out you might be, there will always be things that bring you joy, or a sense of purpose, even if they're very simple. This is where you need to keep your focus when you're trying to find the motivation to take action and get better.

In my life, it has often been my relationships with the animals around me, but it can be anything. Even having a houseplant in your room that you need to water regularly can be enough of a reason to get out of bed and keep going. As long as keeping that house plant thriving brings you a sense of purpose and joy, it's a good reason. Everyone is different, so your reason to stay motivated might be more or less complicated than mine. Yet, you might find that the reason, more often than not, will reside outside yourself as something, or someone, that requires your care.

A great example of a highly motivating reason to keep fighting for your well-being is if you are a parent or guardian and have a child that relies on you. Without you, that child's life would be gravely misfortuned. Or another example is if you have a family member you can think of that would be devastated to lose you and would likely spend the rest of their lives hurting without you, such as a parent, a niece or nephew, a close friend, or a romantic partner. These are extreme examples, but any reason that provokes a strong emotion within you is a good reason to focus on.

It may not be obvious, but I guarantee you there is something or someone in your life worth fighting depression for—sometimes, it can be as simple as not letting the reason for your pain win (in my case, my mother leaving and growing up an undiagnosed autistic). It can be a matter of stating out loud,

 "You do not get to win!"

And directing that at your epicenter of pain. This is where a little bit of anger can work in your favor. Get angry at your pain and use that raw emotion to fight!

Even a positive memory can serve as your reason. For instance, if you have a memory of a time in your life when you weren't struggling, keep this in mind and know that if it was possible once, it will be possible to experience joy like that again. Maybe not in the exact same way, but in a way that is new and even better.

Pain has taught me how to give and connect with others. Giving and connecting in any way are actions that bring us joy. Your pain can have a positive outcome, but you must make a decision, and you must take action. By the way, deciding on a reason is action!

Another example of a good reason is a goal that you want to achieve in your life. Maybe you are studying for a degree, or you are living in a bad neighborhood and have always wanted to move away. You can use a big life goal as your reason to get up every day and fight for the life that you want. If you spend enough time visualizing the life you want, complete with sights, sounds, and smells, you will unconsciously move in that direction. You will embrace and welcome change, allowing space for serendipitous moments to happen, 'luck' will appear in the guise of a new friend, a book like this, or a job offer—if you simply give yourself a reason and stay focused on it, that reason will answer you.

There are so many valuable things that come along with this one simple step. So many aspects of yourself can grow when you just keep opening up your life to the possibilities that lie ahead of you. If you find your reason and get up every day to meet that need, you will set in motion a trajectory of action and change. This is because you are going against the narrative that depression is feeding your mind, and you are forcing a new and better path for yourself.

Whatever it is, you need to have a good reason to keep moving forward so that no matter how bad things get, you always have something to focus your attention on that isn't in line with your depression or anxiety. I still make sure I stay aware of things in my life that bring value, even though I do see the value of just living life for myself as well.

However, when you are stuck and you aren't sure how you are going to find the motivation to keep trying, take this pyramid into account:

This diagram shows the ascending order of focus on your main reasons to keep striving for a better life.

Your daily reasons for getting up in the morning are at the bottom because they are constantly shifting as your circumstances change. They could change quickly, or they can change slowly depending on what they are. For example, getting up daily to feed your cat is a constant, but if you no longer have a cat, your reason will need to shift. If you stay aware of the types of reasons mentioned before, you will find that a new reason reveals itself.

Your big life goals are higher up as they represent bigger shifts and changes in your life that are also going to change as you achieve them. For example, increasing your monthly salary to afford a better life for you and your family. Once that goal is met, the next big life goal will take its place. There is always room to grow, so don't limit yourself when it comes to these.

And finally, at the top, you have your life purpose, which is something that you will continue to work towards your entire life. This is your overall reason for being here on Earth. When you do anything that aligns with this purpose, you will feel more fulfilled. For example, helping others or being a great parent.

Each one of these aspects is important to feeling motivated to take action towards improving your life and feeling better. They are all interlinked as each one connects with what brings you joy in this world.

Knowing your life's purpose is not something you need to fully understand right now, but it is something worth thinking about along your journey toward happiness and self-love. What you *can* do right now is go to your Workbook and complete the exercises provided for you so you have a solid idea of what it is that keeps you motivated to take action in life.

You need to find a reason to get up every morning, no matter how you feel. Something that motivates you through all your suffering to get up, get dressed, and care for yourself. Even if, at first, that is simply getting up to make sure your pet is fed, getting to school to take your favorite class, or getting to work so you can feed your family. In doing so, you will be surprised by the positive impact this can have on your mental well-being.

IT STARTS WITH RESILIENCE

Once you have this reason to get you up every morning, no matter how difficult that may be, you will be training your brain to exercise resilience. Every time you push yourself out of your comfort zone, you become more resilient. Every time you get out of bed when you feel like it's impossible, you become more resilient. And every time you prove to yourself that you can bypass the restrictions depression and anxiety put on your life, you become more resilient.

This will kick off your healing process by teaching you how to do the best thing you can possibly do to make it through anything in life — never giving up.

You will be waking up every morning and trying your best — even if that best is simply getting out of bed and pouring a scoop of kibble into your pet's bowl. As long as you're trying your best, honestly and truly, you can know that you are on the road to recovery. You can be proud of that, no matter what it looks like in comparison to your better days.

This incredible action that you take daily to fight against what the illness of depression or anxiety is telling you slowly blossoms into more and more positivity in your life. You start to embrace the unknown of doing something that scares you, and you open space for curiosity to flex its muscles. Instead of staying frozen in a fear-based state, you begin revealing your vulnerability in a way that uncovers the immense strength that you carry within you.

Then as you bloom in this powerful awareness of what you're capable of, you begin to trust in yourself more and more until you start to KNOW that you can handle whatever life throws at you. You prove to yourself over and over again that you ARE capable and that you CAN take action towards a better future for yourself, even when your mind is telling you that you can't. Your inner voice slowly becomes louder than that of the illness, and you win the battle.

It all starts with that one reason. And, suddenly, you look back and feel astounded by how far you've come. Through this conscious action you take, you start to flourish. Your Workbook has some great activities to help you with this process.

When you are ready and have figured out at least one reason to motivate you to get out of bed and do your best every day, you can officially move on to Part 2! Meet me in chapter 5, and be prepared to learn why you are reading this book in the first place. You are creating a positive shift in your life.

PART 2

What Can I Do Now?

5

THERE IS POSITIVITY IN NEGATIVE EMOTIONS

The secret of change is to focus all of your energy, not on fighting the old, but on building the new.

– Socrates

Dreading the day ahead, I kissed my dad on the cheek and walked towards the school bus. I grabbed onto the railing and stepped up on the platform, then looked around for an open seat. The bus left at 7 am on the dot, and because we lived so far out, I had made it with only a minute to spare. The last seat left open was next to my former best friend.

Mary and I used to be inseparable. We spent every day together and would have a sleepover almost every weekend. I loved sleeping over at her house because she lived two streets up from the beach. Listening to the ocean waves crashing was the perfect lullaby.

I'll admit that her house was an escape for me, as I always felt calm and able to be myself there. Then, out of the blue, her mom refused to allow me over anymore. I was no longer allowed to have sleepovers at their house, and Mary was told to make new friends. I still do not know for sure why this was, but it happened soon after self-harm became an issue in my life. Mary had lost her father the year before she moved to my town, so I've always assumed that her mother was trying to protect her from friends she viewed as "dangerous" influences on her daughter.

This hurt me so much that I became bitter about the situation. I have always been someone who struggles to get close to people and to lose someone that felt like a sister to me was crushing. Especially since the friendship ended without any obvious wrongdoing on my behalf and no explanation given. Anything, even "You're too different for us." might have sufficed, but I was rejected in silence.

Nevertheless, Mary and I continued to spend time together at school, but it wasn't long before she was spending time with new friends she had met at her church's youth group. I was not included in this change. The following year we started our first year of high school together in the same school.

Forced to sit next to Mary on the bus, the resentment that had grown over the summer quickly resurfaced. I ridiculed her for her belief in God and said things that I knew would bring her down. Through all the struggles I had faced and the judgemental looks I would get at church, I had recently discarded my label as a Christian. I felt abandoned by God and unwelcome in the faith I was raised in for being so different.

It did not make me feel better, but the toxicity brewing in my heart spilled over in this moment. Instead of expressing my hurt, I hid behind a tough-girl demeanor. I was by no means a bully, but in this moment, I bullied Mary.

It is not in my nature to bully, and this memory brings me a tremendous amount of shame and guilt. Still, I need you to understand just how noxious mental illness can be so you will fully embrace the positive notions and methods Part 2 has in store for you. With this story, I need you to understand that even if it is not intentional, depression and anxiety can cause a lot of residual damage. The pain of depression and the chaos of anxiety do not often stay within the boundaries of the person suffering. Emotions are contagious, whether we know it or not.

IDENTIFYING WITH NEGATIVE EMOTIONS

After gradually becoming more and more depressed, I became resentful that I was struggling while none of my immediate peers seemed to be. Their lives seemed so normal. Even though Mary had gone through a traumatic experience, her mom was so fierce in her nurturing that Mary's life stayed largely normal, or at least this is what it seemed like from my perspective.

I also had an element of jealousy over the connection Mary had with her mom. I was resentful that she had a mom in her life fighting for her protection and trying to keep her life as stable as possible despite the tremendous loss their family had endured. Throughout our friendship, Mary's family had also quickly grown on me. Her brother and her sister were both such a joy, and I loved them all the same. This made the rejection ever more painful.

By this point, it was very clear that I had a massive amount of negative emotions plaguing my existence. I was experiencing a whirlwind of emotions, from anger, sadness, fear, and emptiness, to grief, resentment, frustration, and self-doubt. I seldom experienced true joy. The best I would feel was a state of calm contentment when I would spend time alone outdoors or around animals.

I quickly started to identify with these negative emotions I experienced so often, and I allowed them to consume my identity. Depression quickly turned to anger, and I was often bad-tempered and sarcastic so that no one would know that I was deeply insecure and fragile underneath it all.

My entire personality and mask became armored for my protection. After all, I believed keeping myself safe was left up to me. My grandmother had no real role in my life yet, and as much as my dad and I had a strong relationship, he did not have the instincts to pick up where my mom left off. My dad always did the best that he could, but at this point in my life, our relationship was based on surface-level conversations and momentary upliftment as he was still learning to cope without her help and struggling with the loss himself. It was one of the darkest times after losing my mom, even though it had already been years.

However, on the bright side, although we didn't often talk about feelings, humor was a strong coping mechanism we both shared on the better days. It is one of the coping skills I have never thrown away as it has allowed me to try not to take life too seriously when possible. It's always good to try and see the silver lining in a bad situation, even if that is just a little bit of humor.

During my depressive dips, I kept up the quiet, tough-girl demeanor and continued with this pattern for most of my high school years. I didn't let many people behind this mask out of fear. I thought that if others viewed me as tough when I was struggling, they wouldn't know how soft I was. I viewed being soft and sensitive as being emotionally weak. This is not true. There is so much power in vulnerability.

It is natural to feel guarded when you are struggling emotionally. Out of instinct, you might feel it necessary to protect yourself or keep up an appearance of strength and toughness. We often don't want others to know how soft or scared we are behind the walls we put up around ourselves. But becoming more vulnerable will allow you to properly process and work through your pain as well as let others know that you might need help.

My success with recovery from mental illness was by no means done alone. The support I have built up in recent years has played a major role in my continued mental health. I am still held accountable for my own coping, but since opening up more and becoming more vulnerable, the people in my life are now fully able to support and encourage my journey. I realized that it was largely my own demeanor, insecurity, and behavior that constantly pushed others away. Now that I have found stability within myself, my relationships with people have grown stronger, longer lasting, and more fulfilling.

There is nothing wrong with needing help or compassion. Nobody can keep up with a facade forever, and a good support system can go a very long way. Better you reveal the truth of how you feel on your terms than wait until your mask is ripped off of you in a moment of despair or extreme difficulty. Eventually, the truth always comes out anyway.

You might even find that once you open up about how you're truly doing, it is what others around you have been waiting for. Those who love us and know us very well can often see through the facades we play up during a bad time. With that said, it is possible to go under the radar and hide your depression very well. How many times have you laughed and smiled only to wipe away tears in the bathroom? But the question you need to start asking yourself is, how is that serving you?

When we struggle emotionally, especially with depression, we have a tendency to shut others out and close off opportunities for others to reach out and support us. This is why depression is known for being an isolating experience. We push others away,  many times unknowingly. This is a dangerous card to play and a habit worth shaking. If you want to expand your support system, the LearnWell Community is a great place to feel less alone.

I need you to be open to your vulnerability so you can make good use of whatever support system you have in your life. Don't make my mistake and shut others out until it's too late. Do it now! Let others into the truth of your struggles now. This will become easier with the steps in chapters 6-8 as I show you how to grow your self-awareness and adopt healthier ways to cope with the ups and downs of life.

BECOMING MORE TRUE TO YOURSELF

Soon, keeping up my mask became a detrimental spiral of what I later realized was autistic burnout caused by the obvious drain of trying to keep up with a neurotypical social life and status. After wearing the mask for as long as I could, I would become emotionally exhausted and lose the energy to keep it up. Maintaining friends was almost impossible when no one really knew who I was. The minute the mask would lift, it was as if I had revealed a hidden tattoo on my forehead saying "damaged goods," and the friends would disappear.

Without the subcontext of knowing I was autistic, the friends around me did not understand what my social deficits meant for the friendship. To them, I came off as suddenly uninterested, disconnected, and unusual when I could normally keep up with them. The truth was that I had suddenly dropped the mask and revealed my hidden discomfort for social intensity. Aka, eye contact like staring contests, perfectly inflected tone like characters from the teenage drama "Mean Girls," and body language that screamed confidence. I just could not keep up with it anymore.

Whenever I feel the need to be emotionally guarded around certain people, the "tough-girl" mask still occasionally makes an appearance to this day. Now that I am learning to unmask completely, I often receive the very labels I was masking to get away from in the first place. "Too sensitive," "Too talkative," "Too much." I'm okay with that. If I am being true to myself, that matters more to me than how others view me. I hope that you can see the value in that. There is no one else you can be better than yourself. You are exactly who you are meant to be, and there is everything right about that! The people around you can only truly love and appreciate you if you show them who you truly are.

In a strange oxymoron type of way, the friends I have made since unmasking and being more true to myself have stuck around longer than any other friends I've ever had before. The "unlovable" version of myself I was hiding from the world has become the very version that draws the right people into my life.

Becoming more true to myself is a big part of my personal healing journey. In these next few chapters, I will show you how you can become more true to yourself, so you can start loving yourself and discover how much potential for healing you truly have.

I do not use the word "journey" lightly, as that is exactly what healing is. It is not something that happens overnight. Healing is a lifelong process. It's going to be lifelong for you too, and that isn't something to be afraid of. My wish for this chapter is to open the doors for a major positive shift to happen in your life by preparing you for the life-changing methods waiting for you in chapters 6, 7, and 8. You need to be open to allowing more light and positivity into your life in order to be happy.

I am not asking you to pretend that negative emotions don't exist. They have a place along your healing journey and in your life. I'm not asking you to disregard your negative emotions and mask them with positive ones. This chapter is about understanding that you have to sincerely nurture a mindset and lifestyle that is conducive to allowing in more positive emotions. You can't be happy if your life is ruled by negativity. It just doesn't make sense. Not for anyone, and not for you.

LETTING GO OF ATTACHMENT

Depression and anxiety can slowly breed negativity in your life and in your mind. If you struggle with either one for long enough, your personality will develop around your experience. Just as a bubbly little girl can turn into a guarded, resentful teenager, poor mental health can negatively impact the essence of who you are. Or, at least, who you show the world. How has mental struggle affected your personality or behavior? This is something worth thinking about throughout this book, as behaviors can either serve you or work against you.

Persistent mental struggle can also turn you into someone you don't identify with. It can open up opportunities for you to spread negativity to others, just like I spread my negativity to Mary that day on the school bus.

If you are inclined to behave in ways that bring others down, it's worth asking yourself why. It is likely that you are unhappy and struggling in a way that makes bringing others down feel rewarding to you – even if it is on an unconscious level.

Eventually, if you have struggled with depression and anxiety for a long time, you can begin identifying with the person you might have become because of your struggles. You might feel attached to certain aspects of your behavior and feel that changing them means losing who you are. This is not true.

Change can be precarious and feel unstable, yet simultaneously necessary. Often we are not sure-footed as we transition from one place of being to the next. The journey can feel uncomfortable. But knowing that change is possible while understanding the goodness in it is the first lamp lighting the way toward who you're truly meant to be. It might start out as a stumble in the right direction, but with conscious redirection of every misstep, soon it will become a sprint.

For example, if you are a humorous person who is often sarcastic during confrontations, you might label yourself as witty. You might identify with being a witty person and become attached to this perceived personality trait. When others react negatively to this behavior, you might say something like, "this is who I am," or something else that deflects the responsibility off of you.

However, if you hurt others by being sarcastic and use it as a way to defend yourself, this might be an unhealthy trait that does not serve you or those around you. Working on becoming less sarcastic and learning better communication skills could help you become a happier person.

This does not mean you are giving up who you are or that you aren't allowed to be yourself anymore. You might have been a naturally funny person until experiencing some trauma, neglect, or abuse that created this unhealthy aspect of humor that finds its punchline in diminishing others. Don't waste time feeling resistant to change or feeling guilty for your behavior. Just start redirecting your missteps now so you can continue on a path to becoming the happy person you want to be.

There was a time when I would gossip with my friends and talk down about others to help me feel some sense of superiority and acceptance. Whenever one of my targets would say or do something I knew these "friends" would find amusing, I would use it to gain popularity with them. I am naturally a talkative person that loves to make people laugh, but this was a horrible toxic trait I had gained out of my own insecurity.

Once I started healing, I had to let go of this trait and all the friends associated with it – at least those who seemed unwilling to grow out of it with me. It was lonely at first as I went through a period of withdrawal from the approval I used to unconsciously seek from others. But with this release of attachment to my negative trait as well as the people and things feeding it, I made space in my life for new friends with a more positive impact on my life. Very soon, better experiences drew me into this renewed version of myself, and I became much happier.

This toxic aspect of my personality slowly shed away, layer by layer, and became replaced with compassion and love for others. I realized that humility was far more valuable than the fleeting rush of others' approval. Now, my talkative nature and desire to uplift my friends are never at the expense of other people.

Try not to become attached to personality traits that do not serve you or others. A bully is not born a bully, and the light of a happy-go-lucky child can become dimmed with trauma. Our experiences can shape us in ways we don't realize. This is why self-awareness is such a vital part of the healing journey. By becoming aware of yourself, including your behaviors and patterns, you can grow and work on yourself to become a better version of YOU.

Once you become aware that aspects of your personality have developed from your experience with depression and anxiety, you will be more receptive to change. You can then let go of any attachments you may have towards this version of yourself you're trying to heal. You have begun to understand the external influence and constructs of being human. Yes, we all carry a core identity, but so much is shaped by our environment. And if your identity can be shaped once, it can be shaped again to better serve you and those around you.

This forms part of the Nature vs. Nurture argument in psychology. That is the argument between whether our behaviors are influenced by genetics, called innate behavior, or environmental influences such as media, parenting, peers, and religious teaching—our so-called learned behavior.

Through my experiences, I believe we are influenced by both. It shouldn't be Nature Vs. Nurture, but rather Nature AND Nurture. The book From Neurons To Neighborhoods[2] states: "Beginning at the moment of conception, hereditary potential unfolds in concert with the environment."

Some of the studies conducted by the book's researchers include the ratio of effect nature and nurture have in various adoption situations, differences between genetically identical twins, and the impact hereditary disorders such as antisocial personality disorder as well as Autism can have on children in different environments.

These studies show that the impact of nature (innate behavior) is greatly influenced by nurture or environmental factors. The two work in concert with each other, with nurture having a significant effect on the severity of hereditary influences. So, just like I have a strong innate tendency towards humor, my trauma (external environment) created a sarcastic and biting edge to my humor that hurt others.

Research conducted about the relationship between nature and nurture concludes that: "The interaction of nature and nurture underscores the importance of creating current conditions of care that respect inherited characteristics, recognizing that nature-nurture is a source of continuing potential change across the life course." In other words, we can change and change for the better.

It shows that we have the ability to shift or improve on negative tendencies associated with our natural behavior. We can unlearn certain behavioral patterns picked up from our environment and work to understand our innate traits so that we can cope with and express these behaviors in a healthier way.

This isn't easy to do as it puts a lot more responsibility in your hands regarding your behavior. It relieves you of the notion that "I am the way I am" and that there's no changing that. Remember, you are responsible for your actions no matter what you've been through, and changing bad behavior is possible.

It is very important that you are able to understand how every aspect of your personality right now, in the swings of anxiety and depression, is not necessarily solid. This is especially relevant if you have been struggling with depression for an extended time. Prolonged negative experiences, and your reactions and behaviors associated with them, can be perceived as part of your core self. But they are not. Most of these behaviors, or at least the exacerbated negative versions of these core behaviors, are more closely linked to nurture rather than nature.

You need to know that this means it IS possible to shift and change certain negative aspects of who you are to grow and become a version of yourself that is thriving and happy. It takes time and conscious redirection of thoughts and actions, but it is possible. Keep reading, and you will get there.

We are constantly shifting and adjusting to the experiences we have along our journey. If we are unaware of the effect circumstances can have on us and do not have the skills to cope, we risk falling victim to prolonged negative emotions that cause the formation of negative personality traits.

You do not have to suddenly become a consistent ray of sunshine and plaster a smile on your face everywhere you go. But you do have to be open to letting go of old patterns in your behavior that might be negatively impacting your life.

You have to be willing to shed the skin that you have built up during the months or years that you've been struggling. You have to be open to discovering a new version of yourself or rediscovering parts of your core self that have been dimmed by the darkness of depression. You are not transforming yourself into someone else. You are simply remembering who you already are beneath the hurt and learned behaviors that are not serving you.

If you want to heal, it requires slowly shifting your mind, your behaviors, and your life to allow for more light and positivity to move into who you are. To combat the negativity that takes you over when you struggle with depression and anxiety, you have to shine the light of awareness on your negative thoughts and behaviors and slowly retrain yourself to live within a more positive framework. This is not a click-of-a-button step. This will take conscious effort in learning methods that will help you "reprogram" any wiring in your brain that isn't serving you.

NURTURING HEALTHY PROGRESS

Following the negative cannabis oil experience with my mother-in-law, I had to restart my recovery from scratch. I also acquired new labels and disorders that I had to add to my recovery quota. However, the one positive thing that came from this experience was that any mask I had on before was now stripped away to a rawness that I had never experienced. It was terrifying, and my identity felt shattered into a million pieces.

But, with the help of my therapist at the time, and regular exposure to horses, I slowly but surely pieced together the truth of who I am. I slowly revealed aspects of my core self that had been overshadowed by illness. I had been given a blank slate to rebuild my life, and instead of becoming bitter again and victimizing myself, I took the opportunity to start my journey toward becoming the best version of myself. Even though we often don't realize it, depression can make us feel like the whole world is against us, and we tend to sink into a victim mentality. Part of recovery is realizing that this is yet another lie mental illness has fed us, and we begin rediscovering our innate strength.

The walls I had up suddenly crumbled down. But instead of digging myself a hole or putting the walls back up, I built myself a stronger foundation to stand on. This is where my true healing journey began, and my life, with all its ups and downs, became a place where my well-being came first.

With each failure and struggle, I have been able to rise above it. I no longer allow myself to stay down when I have fallen. I see a value in myself that I was oblivious to before. I know now that I deserve to put my health first and love myself before I love anyone else. I desperately want you to see that in yourself as well.

My journey to self-love officially began that year, but it is still continuing to this day. As I mentioned, it is a journey, and in my process, I continued to experience great hardships. However, by applying the methods in the chapters to come, I have been able to continue healing and staying above life's challenges in a more productive and positive way. I have surprised myself and my loved ones with my ability to keep moving forward and making progress in my own happiness and success without experiencing the significant lows that I would have had in the past. I want this to happen for you too!

Just like a deep depression or anxiety disorder does not form overnight, recovery from depression and anxiety does not happen overnight either. Recovery is about slowly nurturing ourselves back to health by hitting the rewind button and getting back to some basic fundamentals about our identities. For every negative emotion and behavior, there is a positive way we can shift our reaction or association with it. You can let your emotions control you and become a bain to your existence, or you can shift your emotions to serve you, teach you, and evolve you. It is a matter of releasing attachment and learning to understand that our emotions are not 'fixed' states of being. When we create space to observe our emotions instead of falling victim to them, this is when we can learn from them.

It's up to you to choose, once again, between self-care or self-destruction, love or fear. This is a choice you will have to make over and over again until choosing love becomes more natural to you. At first, it will feel difficult, and you might have to convince yourself why you deserve to choose love. But over time, as you build your self-love and begin to recognize your value, choosing love becomes the obvious choice.

This positive shift is going to happen in your life at a unique pace for you. You may feel like everything just clicks, but it is likely that you will experience a more gradual transformation. Take this graph into account:

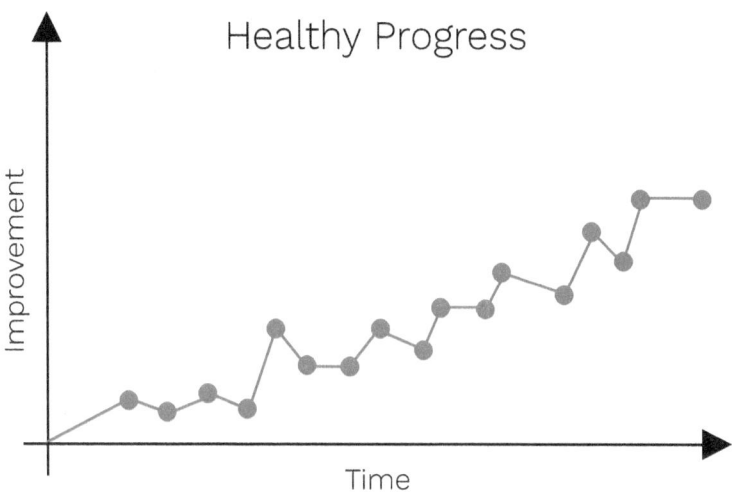

This graph shows what healthy progress can look like. Life is full of ups and downs for everyone, so it is completely normal and healthy to have ups and downs along your journey. There is no good or bad speed to make progress either. Your journey is personal and unique. As long as you are making progress, that is all that matters.

Keep in mind that you are not a failure if you have a dip in your mental health along the way. If you are moving forward, you are making progress. Even if your graph would have bigger dips than the one above, provided you are putting in the work and lifting yourself back up again, you are still making good progress.

However, I am certain that if you apply the methods you are about to learn in the following chapters consistently and to your best ability, your progress will surprise you. And, if you do have a big dip, you will be better equipped to lift yourself back up faster than before.

PRIORITIZING YOU

One of my favorite analogies is the one with a mother and her child sitting in an airplane that is about to crash. Although her instinct is to put the oxygen mask on her child before herself, it is wiser for her to receive oxygen first and then assist her child. She is of better value to others if she has oxygen than if she doesn't reach the mask in time and passes out.

In the same way, I ask you to consider your own well-being as your number one priority. If you are healthy and happy, you will have a more positive effect on those around you and do far more good for others than if you are putting others first and allowing your own energy and well-being to deplete. This is the same notion as

 "You can't pour from an empty cup."

It is not selfish to care about your own health before others; you are of better service to those around you when you are well and happy. This is why I want to say congratulations for getting this far in the book and committing to your healing journey.

You have proven that you are willing to be honest about your well-being and how you are currently coping in your life. You have proven that you are open to embracing new possibilities for your healing. And you have proven that you are prepared and willing to do what it takes to experience the positive shift you need in your life to become the best version of yourself yet.

Now, you are ready to move on and learn the vital, life-transforming methods that you can actively apply in your life to experience a significant positive shift.

Go to your Workbook now and complete the exercises waiting for you so you will be fully prepared to absorb one of the biggest components to a successful healing journey – adjusting your mindset.

You might have heard about what an impact your mindset can have in your life, but I want to show you how the power of your mindset can go from malignant to magic with a few simple changes. Keep an open mind and turn to Chapter 6 after you've completed the exercises in your Workbook.

6

THE MAGIC IN YOUR MINDSET

The true definition of mental illness is when the majority of your time is spent living in the past or future, but rarely living in the realism of NOW.

– Shannon L. Alder n.d

Throughout my journey with mental illness and navigating the world as an undiagnosed autistic, I spent a lot of time growing up feeling like A: Something was missing, and B: The whole world was against me. I spent a lot of time in victim mode.

This caused strife in my life and especially in my relationships with people. I felt like an alien from some distant galaxy, or one of those changeling creatures the fairies switch out human babies for. Many times, I found myself wondering if I was adopted. Something was missing, and I couldn't figure out what it was. I just felt *different*. At least, that's how I felt around others. When I was alone, I was just me.

Once I found out that I was autistic, the feeling that *something was missing* completely melted away. All the dots of my life connected. It was overwhelming in the most incredible way. I mourned the life I thought I should have had for some time, and I still have some letting go to do. But once that tiny, yet profoundly significant, detail of who I am came my way, all that was left was feeling B—*the whole world is against me*. So I started working on changing this narrative for myself. I didn't want to feel like a victim any longer.

We need to switch the focus. Instead of focusing on the past, or your struggles, I want you to focus on a place where we actually spend our lives but often don't take much notice of. No, it is not a heavenly realm or a fantasy land, but it IS where all the magic of transformation happens. That place is the *present*. It is NOW.

Depression and anxiety are not illnesses that exist in the present moment. Depression is an illness that holds all its power in the past, and anxiety is an illness that holds all its power in the future.

Like two villainous sidekicks, they often work hand-in-hand to keep you away from where you hold all the power, and they don't. Can you guess where that is? You're absolutely right - NOW!

The present moment is all that truly is, and once we can grasp that, we can take back all the energy we give away to moments that don't need it anymore. We can recollect and redirect our energy toward building a better present.

CONSCIOUS REDIRECTION OF THOUGHTS

The past is made up of memories and moments that have come and gone. They are over, and they no longer exist in the present. The future is made up of hypotheticals, expectations, and the vastness of the unknown, none of which exist in the present moment either. 'Now' is a state of happening. It is the only constant and most tangible thing we have. This is where we should put our valuable time and energy.

When you focus too much on the past, you stay stuck in your old framework of existence and destine yourself to relive the same patterns and cycles you always have. If you focus too much on the future, worrying about things that could happen, should happen, or would happen, you block off the potential for new possibilities. But when you focus on the present moment, the moment happening right now before your very eyes or ears, you begin building an appreciation for all the good that is already in your life.

Studies conducted on mindfulness practices[3] show that the brain has modifiable neural structures which respond positively to mindfulness training and exercises. In other words, our brains are malleable. The positive effects of practicing mindfulness are proven to last beyond the practice itself and even increase gray matter in the parts of the brain associated with mental well-being, showing improved functioning in those areas. With daily mindfulness practices and meditation, gray matter increase was seen in as little as 8 weeks.

Depression and anxiety keep your awareness in the past and future, ultimately directing your energy to the places that do not govern a positive outcome of your life. Every time you wallow in or attach to an old painful memory, instead of consciously working to look at it more objectively, you strengthen the connection between the neurons in your brain that associate this memory with fear, pain, and stress. But if you can work to become more mindful and aware of your present moment, you can consciously redirect your thoughts and emotions associated with a painful memory changing the way you experience that memory in the present moment.

For example, suppose you become lost in the remembrance of a painful breakup. In that case, you will ignite the neurons in your brain, leading to the emotional reaction you have always associated with that memory. You will trigger the same pain, anger, and grievances you have always held onto about this memory. But, if you consciously redirect your thoughts, your emotions will follow. Redirect, as in, tweak and shift them to fit a more realistic narrative. Soon your brain will begin building a new, more productive chain of reactions associated with the memory, thereby shifting your emotions.

This is a fancy way of saying that <u>you can change the narrative in your mind to serve you rather than hurt you.</u> Your thoughts are not concrete; they are trainable with conscious redirection. You can shift your mindset to view life through a lens that heals you instead of one that keeps you stuck in the pain of the past.

Whenever you are experiencing an emotion, there are likely thoughts that preceded them. A sudden pang of emotional pain in your heart could have been triggered by the thought, "Nobody loves me." Or, you could suddenly feel relief after thinking, "Everything's going to be okay." By paying attention to the thoughts that trigger an emotion, rather than being consumed by the emotion itself, you give yourself the power to shift the moment in a more productive direction.

Emotions often govern how we enjoy or experience life. So if your emotions are running wild, you can reign them in by taking more responsibility over your thoughts. You don't always have to change the thought completely; just rearrange it to fit a more objective outlook. Objectivity is the key to taking bad things that happen less personally.

With my divorce, instead of allowing my thoughts and emotions to run away with me, I consciously decided to redirect my thoughts in a more objective light, letting go of my personal attachment to the situation. Instead of thinking, "How could he do that to me?" and wallowing in the self-loathing thoughts that I was having, I chose to start replacing that thought with something like, "We were both young, and we both made mistakes. It's over now."

Consciously redirecting your thoughts in this way builds a new narrative in your mind that does not give away your power to a victim mentality. It's okay to feel hurt over a painful memory, but you can use this conscious redirection to better process the memory and build up a more objective narrative about the situation. This will release your subjective attachment to it and reduce the intensity of the emotions triggered by it.

So if you find yourself having a thought that has triggered an unpleasant emotional reaction, simply follow up that thought with your conscious redirection. You can think, "Nobody loves me." And then follow up the thought with something like, "That's probably not true, but it's just how I feel in this moment."

The more you practice conscious redirection of thoughts, the more it becomes second nature. You will begin to automatically identify which thoughts triggered your emotion and fact-check whether or not they are fair. Over time, it will become much easier to stay objective about negative situations, and you will be able to keep your peace.

ALL POSSIBILITIES LIE IN THE UNKNOWN

Reclaiming your power over memories of the past and fears of the future does not take away the painful things that have happened to you. But it is a way of reminding yourself that you are safe now; the moment is over. You do not need to relive that moment anymore.

The same thing happens when we focus on a fictionalized future outcome of a situation: we give away our energy to this hypothetical scenario instead of putting our valuable energy, time, and action into making a better outcome possible. We close ourselves off to the greatness of the unknown and hold our awareness to an outcome that isn't real and likely never will be.

The past is often the trigger for future hypotheticals. We generally only fear things in the future based on what we have already experienced. But the past does not govern the future if you don't let it. Focusing your awareness on and spending more time actively pursuing the present moment slowly weakens your attachment to the past. We can open our minds up to the possibilities waiting for us instead of creating a fictionalized outcome.

Embracing the uncertainty of the unknown allows it to spark your wonder rather than fear. Not knowing what is going to happen doesn't need to be a negative thing. If life was always predictable, there would be no room for surprise or excitement. I believe that the unknown is not called great because it's vast but because it's *great,* as in amazing!

Embracing the present and letting go of the fear of the unknown releases expectations that limit you and allows for amazing, serendipitous things to happen in your life. Your mindset shifts into a more positive, curious framework, and you start to notice more and more of the good that is in your life. Right here, right now, I promise you it is there.

A present moment to appreciate can be as little as realizing that you're breathing! You're alive, and that is the most wonderful thing in and of itself. You have access to this book! You have access to knowledge, help, guidance, and connection to me as I write these words. You are part of a great world that, although it holds a lot of pain, also holds a lot of joy. You have a choice on where you put your focus. Again, you have to choose: Love or fear?

Most negative emotions do not exist in the present moment. Negative emotions are attached in some shape or form to moments of the past. Even anxiety is ultimately rooted in the past as we fear what might happen based on what we have already experienced. Once you know that that is all negative emotions are, you can begin working to understand where they are rooted and move through them instead of letting them govern your actions and thoughts.

TAKE BACK THE STEERING WHEEL

One of the most profound lessons that I have learned along my journey is that your thoughts create your reality. The more you repeat a thought in your mind, the more you assign truth to it by strengthening the neurons in your brain regarding that thought. This can mean the difference between your thoughts ruling your life and you taking back your rightful position in the driver's seat. You need to take responsibility for the direction you go by taking care of which thoughts you give precedence.

For example, if you think, "I don't fit in," and every time you have an awkward social interaction, a confrontation, or deal with rejection, you think, "I don't fit in," you reinforce that as a truth for yourself. This is also an example of not realizing that thoughts are not always facts. Our minds can blurt out thoughts that simply aren't true, even if, to us, they feel true in that moment.

As you now know, the trouble with letting your thoughts run wild is that thoughts create an emotional reaction within your body, no matter how small they are. The link between thoughts and emotions is a bit like the chicken and the egg debate, as in which one came first? The truth is, they play on each other. A thought can trigger an emotional reaction, and an emotion can provoke a thought.

Depression and anxiety grow their roots deep within your mindset and take hold of the steering wheel of your thoughts. This is how they gain power over you and govern your life. They provoke thoughts that feel like your own but are secretly lies conjured up by the illness. Thoughts like "You're not good enough," "You don't belong anywhere," or "The world is better off without you." Painful thoughts like these provoke painful emotions that keep you a slave to your own body and mind.

Our power lies in realizing that we can take back control over our thoughts and can therefore control our emotions, slowly unbinding ourselves from the clutches of depression and anxiety. But how do you control thoughts? Cue mindfulness!

Mindfulness can slowly transform your mindset by training your mind to stay aware of itself. It will allow you to better control your thoughts and put the steering wheel back into your hands. One of the most challenging aspects of practicing mindfulness is learning how to detach from your thoughts and, therefore, your emotions as well. Neither thoughts nor emotions define who you are. They are simply products of our experiences.

No matter how hard we try, thoughts inevitably pop into our minds at some stage, even when we are deep in a mindful state, meditation, prayer, or another awareness-consuming activity. Part of practicing mindfulness is learning to release attachment to thoughts and continue returning your mind to a state of peaceful awareness.

WIN THE BATTLE WITH MINDFULNESS

There are many ways that you can practice mindfulness, and there are many benefits to doing this. Yes, mindfulness has become very popular and is a topic becoming more common in the mental health scene, but there is a reason for that – it works!

Benefits include reduced anxiety, improved ability to view the world more objectively, improved mood, and improved cognitive ability. However, one of the most important benefits of mindfulness is that it provokes a state of gratitude within us.

Gratitude for the present moment helps lift the veil of sorrow and despair and slowly replaces it with a lens of unconditional love. It allows you to see the good in places you never could before and helps keep you focused on the light in the toughest of times.

With gratitude comes a more loving and objective outlook. You begin to realize that everyone is just doing their best with what they know, and you release judgment. The unconditional love begins to span across all people, all creatures, and yourself. It happens gradually, but it happens.

You start to realize that we are all just human and that all pain is rooted in the past. If someone did something that hurt you, it came from a place of hurt or fear within them. Mindfulness can help you shift your vision from victim to victor. But you are not the victor over anyone else; you are the victor over yourself. Your own mind is the only thing that you are up against. And mindfulness is the weapon that you can use to win the battle.

HOW TO PRACTICE MINDFULNESS

A simple way to start practicing mindfulness is to pay attention to which activities completely consume your focus. Maybe that is engaging in arts and crafts or playing a sport that you love. Engaging in a hobby or activity that consumes your focus in a positive way, making time slow down, is a form of being in the present moment and, therefore, the perfect place to start practicing mindfulness.

All you have to do in this case is let go and allow the activity to consume you. Fully embrace the moment and release thoughts unrelated to the activity. Try this next time you are engaged in an activity that you love.

In my life, going for a ride with my horse completely centers me in the present moment. When I am on the back of a horse, there is no room to think about other things. My attention is engrossed in every movement the horse makes as I need to stay aware of our surroundings and any potential dangers that we might face. Horses are also very unpredictable animals, and the back of a horse is no place to daydream when you are navigating a jump course or rocky terrain. My mind can release external stressors, and I can fully embrace the moment. I have now found multiple activities that can center me, as horse riding can. I suggest you just start with one activity and see how much mental relief it brings.

The next step to advancing your mindfulness practice is to start actively practicing mindfulness during mundane activities. It's easy to be happy and enjoy the moment when you're doing something you love, but this exercise of practicing mindfulness during a mundane activity is more true to the concept of mindfulness and will deepen your practice in a profound way.

What you need to do is completely focus your awareness on the mundane activity that you're doing and take in every sensation of the task. For example, if you are sweeping the floor, acknowledge and release any thoughts that come into your mind, then focus your awareness on the sensations and sounds of sweeping the floor.

You might focus on the woosh of the broom against the tiles, the feeling of the handle within your palms, the dust particles floating in the sunbeam shining across the room, and the smell of the air as the fresh air replaces the dust.

Allow your mind to be completely consumed by the single task at hand, and use your senses to bring you deeper into this state of awareness. Your senses are a valuable tool in bringing your awareness back to the present moment. Senses are only active in the now.

When you think of a memory or have a negative thought, these events are largely isolated within your mind. Your senses have no role in the past or future. But your senses are fully active in the present moment. Slowly focus your attention on each of your basic senses to pull you out of any state that isn't present. Your five basic senses include:

- Sight
- Sound
- Smell

- Taste
- Touch

This is what we call grounding, and it is the basic practice of bringing your awareness back to your physical senses. Maintaining this state of conscious awareness of the present and holding your awareness here is mindfulness.

You can practice mindfulness in any way that works for you. Simply follow these basic steps to bring yourself into a state of mindfulness during any activity:

> Step 1: Take a deep breath and exhale slowly as you focus on your breathing. Continue breathing deeply and slowly throughout this exercise.
>
> Step 2: Begin focusing your awareness on each of your five basic senses, one by one. You will reach a more present state.
>
> Step 3: Hold your awareness in this present state until you naturally have a thought.
>
> Step 4: When you have a thought, acknowledge the thought without judgment.
>
> Step 5: Release the thought and bring your awareness back to your breath.
>
> Step 6: Repeat.

Thoughts are not dangerous, but our reactions to them and behaviors associated with them can be harmful. This is why you have to learn to allow thoughts to flow without the emotional attachment. Once you master doing that, your thoughts have no power over you. Depression and anxiety then begin to fade as their power lies in your thoughts and emotions before translating to behavior.

You can practice this simple technique during your basic household chores, during that art project you've been working on, or sitting at the foot of your bed in meditation or prayer. Simply use it to come back to the present moment when you wander off into the past or the future without your consent.

Whichever way you can incorporate mindful moments into your daily life, do it. Very soon, mindfulness will become an integral part of your being and help you build a more peaceful life.

JOURNALING FOR INNER PEACE AND SELF-AWARENESS

The powerful state of self-awareness that mindfulness nurtures within you allows you to recognize when you are experiencing symptoms of depression or anxiety before they have rooted themselves in your being.

You might still experience symptoms of depression or anxiety from time to time. But you can nip them in the bud before they progress using mindful self-awareness. You can identify and process the things that trigger you to spiral down before depression or anxiety can take hold.

In Chapter 2, you identified things in your life that were causing your state of being at the time. However, remember, small things can also cause an unequivocal emotional reaction within you. These small things are called triggers. They can be anything that creates a negative chain of events for you, starting with a painful emotion, followed by a negative thought spiral, and then potentially symptoms of depression or anxiety.

For example, someone might call you a mean name, like "stupid," during an argument that triggers a deep emotional reaction within you related to a past trauma. Your thoughts immediately spiral out of control because the word holds emotional weight for you. It then causes an out-of-context experience in the present. You potentially fixate on being called "stupid" and allow it to affect your self-esteem.

Triggers are different for everyone, and they are often rooted in traumatic memories or deep-seated insecurities within us. Nonetheless, mindful self-awareness can help unravel this chain of events and give you a stronger footing when a trigger arises. It gives you a chance to acknowledge and work through the trigger before it can progress into something more.

Your triggers will become more apparent to you as you move forward with your mindfulness practice. The more you spend time in the present moment, staying aware of yourself, your thoughts, and your emotions, the more clarity you will get regarding what your triggers are. Once you recognize a trigger, you can work to unravel it step by step. You can acknowledge it and use conscious redirection to change the narrative around the trigger, slowly dissolving it.

While the practice of mindfulness is very simple, it is surprising how difficult it can be in an emotional moment, especially the more erratic your thoughts are at the time. If your thoughts are too erratic and you are struggling to reach a present state after encountering a trigger, there are ways to regain control over your thoughts and emotions.

One of the best ways to quiet your mind and allow you to reach a more present state of awareness is to journal your thoughts. You can also type them out if you prefer, but I find using a pen and paper helps to engage more of your senses and avoid unnecessary distractions.

Remember, thoughts and emotions are connected. That's why we've created the Workbook for you— to release uncomfortable emotions and better understand your triggers. There are many ways that you can approach the practice of journaling.

One of the most popular journal techniques is following journal prompts. You can play around and try different journal prompts and exercises, and you can also stick to a set of journal prompts to answer daily. These prompts are usually simple questions that provoke specific trains of thought to induce an emotional release or reaction.

Go to your Workbook now and see some examples of what journal prompts can look like. You can use any of the prompts there regularly or search for new ones to try as you go.

Another journal technique that I personally use is entering a flow state and simply scribbling out whatever comes to mind. Most of the time, you don't even know what you're writing until it's on the page. This is a great example of an exercise that can help you release and work through difficult emotions. You'll find all the resources you need to start this practice in the Workbook we have provided for you.

As an autistic person, I often struggle to understand how I feel about a situation, and triggers can often spiral me into a meltdown. It takes me longer to process my feelings, even though they can be very intense and feel very loud on the inside. When I feel an overwhelming, intense emotion that I don't understand and sometimes don't know the trigger of, I write about it in my journal.

Once I'm done, I can read through what I've written and better figure out what emotions are present in the big tornado of feelings I'm having. This often reveals the source of my frustration as well. I look out for patterns and slowly unravel each feeling from the other as I write and read the entry.

If I have had a meltdown and feel confused about the trigger, I use this method of journaling to uncover where things went wrong. This also allows me to look back on previous journal entries to pick up on any patterns or triggers for meltdowns in the past, allowing me to avoid them better in the future.

Meltdowns are such an integral part of the autistic experience, and they are the reason I began to seek a diagnosis in the first place. I knew something was different about me, but I brushed it all off as part of depression, anxiety, and simply being a teenager. However, as I grew up and began to deal with more responsibilities, from paying bills, driving a car, doing my own grocery shopping, and maintaining a healthy romantic relationship, meltdowns became a more frequent and obvious problem in my life.

They are a confusing, overwhelming, and frankly alarming experience for anyone to have, no matter what age you are. Journaling is one of the ways that helps me keep track of what coping skills work to negate this disruptive symptom. It helps me move past the confusion around the event and helps me recognize my triggers so I can work on avoiding them or staying aware of them. It is one of the things that allows me to thrive in my life as an autistic person.

TWO SIDES OF THE SAME COIN

Journaling and mindfulness are two sides to the coin of a positive mindset. They both work to nurture better introspection, better clarity of thoughts and emotional triggers, and better mental attitude towards life's difficulties. Both these practices work to put you in the driver's seat of your life and reduce your subconscious need to be a victim of your circumstances. Both these practices can be used to increase your gratitude for life.

A very popular and effective journaling prompt that you can do daily to amplify your success with mindfulness practices is the gratitude exercise. This exercise works best in a state of mindfulness, and the two amplify each other's effectiveness. All you have to do is add one journal prompt to your daily morning or evening routine. I recommend mornings for this to help start your day off on a positive note and set your mind up for a more conscious day.

The journal prompt for gratitude is this:

 *Write down 10 things you are grateful for in your life.*

You can simply copy the prompt down on your personal journal page each day or use this book's Workbook on the pages where the prompt is already ready and waiting for you. Use this simple daily journaling exercise to shift your mindset towards a state of gratitude for your life that will unlock magic you never knew existed.

Just this one simple journaling exercise can do wonders for a struggling mind. Imagine how much more magic and power is waiting for you with consistent daily mindfulness and journaling practice. Remember, the future is nothing but potential. So embrace the unknown and be open to trying new things!

The only downside to practicing mindfulness and journaling is that they require conscious effort to do the work—at least at first. With time, it becomes easier and more natural. The trick is remembering these practices in times of stress. I know you're willing to do the work already, so just take it in your stride and navigate these incredible yet simple practices into your daily routine. Allow them to become healthy habits in your life.

You can remind yourself to use these incredible tools by leaving reminders for yourself in places where you know you will see them in times of stress. For example:

- Stick a sticky note on your mirror to remind you to breathe and be present.

- Change your phone's wallpaper to something that makes you think of the practice.

- Memorize a mantra or phrase like "Peace is within me, my thoughts do not control me." and repeat it to yourself as often as possible so that it is fresh in your mind when a trigger arises.

- Keep your Workbook on hand as much as you can so that it is already with you if something happens.

- Draw or find a picture of a symbol that reminds you of being mindful, such as a white dove, the Om symbol, or a religious symbol that resonates with you.

- Schedule time in your day to practice mindfulness and journaling to make them a habit in your life.

Practicing mindfulness in any shape or form is a great example of a healthy coping mechanism, also known as a coping skill. These practices used daily can improve your outlook on life or help you get through a tough time more smoothly.

Coping skills are an integral part of learning to float when you feel like you're drowning. They can make or break which direction you go during a tough time. Poor coping skills can keep you spiraling down, while good coping skills can help you rise above the storm. You've come this far, which shows me you are determined to live a life of self-love, so let's keep going. Chapter 7 is all about coping skills and how you can make them work for you instead of against you.

7

THERE'S HOPE WHEN YOU CAN COPE

Those who wish to sing, always find a song.

– Swedish Proverb

Sitting on the floor next to my freshly made bed, I called my sister in a panic. She was working abroad at this time, and I was still in our hometown, struggling to cope with the pressures of an undiagnosed adult life. She answered the phone and could immediately hear that something was off.

This was only a few years after my divorce and I was still getting myself back up on my feet. Bursting into tears, I explained that I was battling to keep my head above water financially and had an important bill to pay. Both my new partner and I were still in the phase of building up our careers. She explained that the money would take a while to come through but that she could help me out with the bill. As reluctant as I was to accept financial help, I had no choice and felt grateful for the relief that came from knowing that I would be able to make the payment. Before my diagnosis, I struggled to keep my life from unfolding into chaos. We had calls like this fairly often at the time, where I found myself in emotional distress, unable to pull myself out without help.

We carried on talking as I offloaded all the things I was worried about in my life. I told her I was trying my best, but I still felt like every day was a battle to keep myself afloat. After a thoughtful pause, my sister offered me a valuable piece of advice that I still reflect on to this day. She said to ask yourself one thing when you feel overwhelmed about a situation,

"Can I change it?"

If the answer is yes, start taking steps toward resolving the problem. And if the answer is no, change your mindset about it.

Can I change it?

As you learn how to cope with stress, anxiety, and depression, you will likely have to face overwhelming situations that make you feel stuck. Instead of letting the situation get the better of you, causing your mind to spiral into a state of panic, start by asking yourself this one simple question.

Ask yourself if you can change it, and if the answer is no, shift your approach to coping with having to accept it. But if the answer is yes, choose coping skills that will allow you to take more positive action toward resolving it.

For example, if you have student loans and are under financial strain, this is something that you can change. Instead of letting yourself get caught up in the stress, start taking steps towards resolving your debt. Even if the progress is slow, you can put your mind at ease, knowing that you are doing something about your problem.

On the other hand, if you are grieving the loss of a loved one, a loss isn't something you can change. So instead of letting yourself become overwhelmed and stuck, start taking steps toward processing and accepting this great loss in your life. You could try grievance counseling or spend time doing things you and your lost loved one used to enjoy together. You can allow yourself to feel sad and go through the grieving process.

This will eliminate the feeling that you're spiraling out of control and put you back in the driver's seat about the situation. Remember to stay in the moment and work on incremental steps. Focusing on the potential outcome of a situation will keep you locked in anxiety.

Also, worrying about something changes nothing; you have to take action to resolve your problems. And if you approach every problem with this question, "Can I change it?" you can avoid feeling stuck and work through difficult circumstances much quicker.

However, for this technique to be effective, you need to have a solid set of coping skills in place. Without good coping skills, you are more likely to spiral into a negative frame of mind and will keep feeling stuck despite your efforts to cope. Good coping skills are part of the foundation for overcoming obstacles quickly and productively.

ALL ABOUT COPING SKILLS

Good coping skills can mean the difference between getting through a bad time unscathed and falling into a depression every time things go wrong. They are the behaviors and actions we consciously take to help us deal with stress. While they do become ingrained in our behavior, like a habit or ritual used for coping, they still require us to make a conscious decision to take action.

Coping skills are learned behaviors we pick up throughout our lives from our parents, peers, the media, and our own trial and error. Although they can be learned at any age, the foundation of whether your coping skills are good or bad generally originates from your childhood role models.

For example, according to studies[4], if you had parents with a substance use disorder growing up, the likelihood of you using drugs or alcohol as a coping mechanism is far higher. On the other hand, if you witnessed your parents coping with stress in healthier ways, like going for a walk or calling a friend, you are more likely to cope with stress in similar ways.

Before reaching adolescence, I had already met peers who had engaged in self-harming behaviors like burning themselves with lighters, using razors to cut their wrists, and scratching themselves. Then, my sister began self-harming for a short period in her early teens. I did not consciously know at the time where the idea came from, but the concept of inflicting harm on myself to find relief was already planted in my mind years before I tried it. It stayed in my subconscious, ready to resurface at my most vulnerable time.

Self-harm and substance abuse are already two great examples of self-destructive coping mechanisms. More examples of poor coping skills include:

- Overeating or undereating
- Reckless behavior (Unsafe sex, speeding)
- Impulsive spending
- Oversleeping
- Avoiding problems
- Playing the victim

The trouble with having poor coping skills is that you are not well-equipped to handle the natural ebb and flow of life. Without a well-rounded toolbox of coping skills to whip out when things get tough, you are far more likely to struggle with depression or anxiety.

Good coping skills allow you to better process and handle the difficult emotions that come along with life's hardships and trauma. And the good news is that if you find yourself relying on poor coping skills, it is not a permanent problem. Good coping skills can be learned, and bad coping skills can be unlearned or replaced. Remember, your brain is malleable. Coping skills are learned behaviors seated in the brain that can be shifted with conscious redirection of your thoughts, emotions, and actions.

KNOWING WHAT WORKS FOR YOU

Walking through the store with my one hand on the side of the grocery cart, the sound of all the people began to amplify and blend with the loud Christmas music blaring across the aisles. Grocery stores are still overstimulating for my senses, but as a young child, I struggled to control my reaction to the overload.

The beeping sound of products being scanned at check-out, the cart wheels squeaking and scratching along the floor, and the loud whirring of the weird aircon pipes covering the store ceiling are my kryptonite. Not to mention ladies wearing strong perfume and the smell of burnt oil in the cooked food section.

Very quickly, I felt the energy build within my little body. The intensity of the sounds all blended into one loud crescendo, and I started moving my body nervously in an unconscious attempt to release the feeling. Raising and dropping my shoulders, squeezing and releasing in a comforting rhythm, I felt the intensity begin to feel more bearable.

Then, with a firm grip on the back of my neck, my mother glared down at me and told me to cut out whatever I was doing. The strange movements were attracting attention, and she was blushing with embarrassment. I forced myself to be still and tried to "behave," but the minute I stopped the movements, the world started to blur into a chaotic jumble of sounds, lights, and overwhelm again. It quickly became too much, and a "tantrum" ensued.

Without knowing that I was autistic, my mom didn't understand that these movements were an integral part of her young daughter's coping and happiness. She did not know that she was unknowingly robbing her daughter of an autistic necessity. I can't blame her either, as the way people stared must have been mortifying for her, especially if she herself was not sure what was going on with me.

However, these strange movements were not bad behavior or hyperactivity. They were self-stimulatory behaviors, also known as stimming. I needed these behaviors in order to release energy and cope with overwhelm.

Without knowing how important stimming was for me and punishing me for the meltdowns that followed, meltdowns very soon became shutdowns. This is where I started completely shutting off from the world in moments of stress and became stuck in a selectively muted, timid state for hours or days on end. This was also the beginning of my journey with masking my true self and true feelings.

For autistics, coping skills can look very different than they do for allistics. Allistic people are not autistic. If you are on the spectrum, it is very important to allow yourself to cope in ways that are healthy for autistic people, such as stimming and engaging in special interests. Special interests are specific interests that autistic people fixate on and indulge in that bring a lot of joy and excitement to our lives. The stereotypical example is a little boy who is obsessed with trains, but in truth, it can be anything. A special interest can even be something that is typical and age-appropriate but is most often taken to the extreme.

However, even if you are not autistic, everyone has individual coping needs that require an understanding of what works best for them. It is so important to find what positive coping skills work for you because that is how you will become better equipped to handle the stressors of life in the most effective way.

POSITIVE COPING SKILLS

In general, the most effective type of positive coping skills are emotion-focused coping skills. These have been found to have the most positive impact and can be split into two approaches: A distraction approach and a processing approach.

Distraction

A distraction approach works by temporarily distracting you from the stress to give you the space and time you need to come down from the emotional reaction associated with the stress. You get a chance to breathe and recalibrate while doing something uplifting.

For example, if you have received distressing news and are stuck in an emotional state, you can watch an uplifting movie, play with your pet, or listen to someone else tell a story instead of immediately addressing the problem.

Distraction is a great tool for coping with anxiety as it removes you from the moment that might have triggered or worsened your symptoms. This allows your body the chance to regulate itself. Once you have successfully distracted yourself from the stress and are in a more regulated state of being, you will be in a better mental space to address the problem or move on with your life in a better frame of mind.

Here is a list of positive distraction methods that you can either identify in your own coping or add to your coping toolbox:

- Focus on your breathing
- Ground yourself
- Practice mindfulness
- Go for a walk outdoors
- Exercise
- Read a book
- Play uplifting music
- Dance
- Start doing chores
- Spend time with an animal

- Watch an uplifting movie or series
- Draw or paint
- Look up inspirational quotes
- Engage in play (ex. board game, bubbles, ball)
- Ask a friend how they're doing
- Practice self-care

Using distraction methods is about temporarily breaking out of a negative or overwhelming mental space. Once you feel more stable, you will be in a better position to process your stress. It is not about avoiding your problems but rather taking a break from thinking about them until you are in a better mental space to face them.

Processing

A processing approach to positive coping includes techniques focused on processing the stressful emotions you are dealing with in the moment. These techniques help you figure out triggers for future reference.

You can use this coping strategy to better understand what went wrong in a stressful situation, like an argument or meltdown. And you can also use it to figure out what went right so that you can use that information to have a better experience if you are faced with a similar situation in the future.

For example, if you get into a fight with your friend and feel emotionally charged afterward, you can choose to process the situation immediately by pinpointing how you feel and what exactly caused you to feel that way. This coping approach will help you understand the cause of the fight and how you can resolve the emotions you are feeling.

You can also use a processing approach after you have used a distraction approach. Once you have been able to cope with the initial overwhelming emotions, you can use a processing strategy to work through what happened.

Here is a list of positive processing techniques that are a great asset to any coping skill toolbox:

- Write about what happened in your journal
- Call or message a friend you can confide in
- Follow a gratitude journal prompt
- Try problem-solving journal prompts
- List out the negative things that you did when handling the stressful situation, followed by what you could have done instead for a better outcome
- Look at a chart of emotions and see which ones you identify with
- Write a letter to a past version of yourself that was hurting
- Write an email or letter to someone that you are upset with, putting all your unfiltered emotions into the letter, then delete or burn it
- Meditate or pray about the problem
- Talk to a trusted therapist

Any activity that allows you to actively work through your emotions and thoughts in a safe, positive, and private setting is a great option for a processing approach to positive coping. You might not always feel completely better after doing a processing activity, but you will most likely feel like a weight has been lifted off your shoulders as you release the heavy emotions you were dealing with.

While distraction methods work to alleviate your symptoms of stress in the moment, processing methods are more effective for long-term relief and coping. However, together, these two coping techniques work substantially well, giving you the tools you need to cope with stressors and overcome depression or anxiety in a healthy, more productive way.

COPING SKILLS FOR AUTISTICS

Imagine a set of coping skills like a set of tools in a toolbox. If you are a plumber, your tools are going to be different from an electrician. Just like different professions require different tools to do the job correctly, different coping skills will work better for different neurotypes. Each of our toolboxes will be unique.

For autistic people, there are a few coping skills unique to the condition and essential for a happy life. Some examples of positive coping skills unique to people with Autism and a few other forms of neurodivergence include:

> **Stimming:** Hand-flapping, spinning in circles, wiggling, and vocalizations. These are ways autistic people can express overwhelming emotions like intense fear, sadness, or even

happiness. They each entail moving the body in a specific way or making a repetitive sound that feels comforting for the person.

Engaging in special interests: Many autistic people have a specific topic of interest that brings them immense joy. The stereotyped special interests for autistic people include an obsession with trains, insects, or mathematics. But they can be anything from a specific cartoon or movie to something "typical" like sports or fitness. What sets an autistic special interest apart from a typical interest is the intense level of passion and enthusiasm to engage in the one topic or activity.

Talking about special interests to others: Simply talking about a special interest can be extremely fulfilling and uplifting for an autistic person, making it a great distraction approach.

Releasing eye contact: Eye contact can be an incredibly uncomfortable experience for an autistic person. Releasing eye contact during a stressful situation can allow you to regain some control over your emotions if you find eye-contact overwhelming.

Playing with sensory toys or items: Sensory stimulation is another form of stimming that helps engage the senses and improve relaxation. Sensory toys, or stim toys, are a great way to get this sensory play in during stressful situations. Stim toys and other sensory items include plush toys, fidget toys, weighted blankets, essential oils, and more.

Fidgeting: Fidgeting is often seen as a bad habit, but for autistic people letting yourself fidget is a good way to help you cope with uncomfortable feelings. It can include repeatedly stroking or feeling the material of your clothes, folding up a napkin while you sit at the dinner table, or straightening out the things on the table.

Wearing protective earwear: Many autistic people are sensitive to noise stimulation, and it can cause an already stressful situation to bubble over into a meltdown. This is why wearing protective earwear can help lower the impact of a situation for an autistic person. Protective earwear includes ear plugs, ear muffs, noise-canceling headphones, or even certain hats that cover your ears.

Changing into comfortable clothes: Simply changing out of tight or scratchy clothing and wearing something more comfortable can be pleasantly stimulating during a stressful situation.

Adjusting lighting to create more ambiance: Bright lights can also increase the intensity of an already difficult situation for autistics. Turning down the lights and allowing for more ambient lighting when you are stressed can significantly improve your coping abilities if light is an issue for you.

Taking some time to be alone: A classic characteristic of Autism is social deficits, making social interaction potentially stressful. Time alone can help autistic people unwind and process how they are feeling without the added stress of reading another person's emotions.

Using a pen and paper to communicate: Selective mutism is another way autistic people might need to cope after a stressful event. Using a pen and paper, or a communication device, to share your needs and feelings with others is a great way to get through a tough time quicker and still feel supported by others.

I want to stress that these are *positive* coping skills for autistic people because many of these needs are confusing to others and sometimes misunderstood as rude. These coping mechanisms are not negative and should rather be embraced as part of the needs of a happy neurodivergent person. They are also not exclusive to Autism. Other forms of neurodivergence, such as ADHD and OCD, might have similar coping needs. It is also possible to benefit from some of these coping skills if you are allistic.

I also want to stress that not all autistic people have the same needs. For example, not all autistic people struggle with selective mutism, a common symptom of Autism where the person can't communicate in certain high-stress situations. Someone with selective mutism would benefit from using a pen and paper to help cope with their difficulties communicating. In contrast, another autistic person with severe sensory processing problems might benefit more from wearing protective earwear. Everyone is unique.

The only coping mechanism unique to Autism that I recommend avoiding is masking your Autism and autistic needs. If you need to put the lights down because they are "too loud," don't be afraid to make your environment more bearable for you. If you need to go home early from a social gathering because your social battery is shorter than your peers, honor your needs.

The right people will understand and accept you exactly the way you are. And if the people you are around don't want to be considerate despite understanding your differences, then focus your attention on finding people that do.

BUILD YOUR COPING TOOLBOX

After looking at all the various positive coping skills available to you, think about your most recent bad time. Think about the things you did to try and cope with the situation as best you could. How did you feel afterward? Were they positive coping skills, or were they self-destructive thoughts and behaviors?

Go to your Workbook now and write down your top 10 most used coping skills. Score them each from 1-10, with 1 being harmful and 10 being very beneficial. Pay attention to any coping mechanisms that are destructive.

One by one, you want to start replacing the harmful coping mechanisms with positive coping skills. This will allow you to overcome challenges much faster and in a more productive way. You don't have to do this overnight or beat yourself up if you make a mistake; just slowly nurture more positive coping within your life.

Self-harm was one of my most destructive coping mechanisms growing up. Even with therapy, it took me years to stop doing it. Self-harm became such a normal part of my life that I still felt the urge every time things got tough. However, when I learned that I was autistic and slowly unmasked to allow for the behaviors I used to shame myself for, that incessant urge completely disappeared.

Now, when I feel extremely overwhelmed, instead of shutting down and wanting to self-harm as a way to release the energy, I allow myself to express the emotions as they come to better process them. I allow myself to stim if I need to, dim the lights if I need to, and wear protective earwear if I need to. Knowing what positive coping looks like for me has been one of the most vital skills I have acquired along my journey.

Spend time figuring out what positive coping skills work best for you, and slowly build your coping toolbox. That way, whenever you feel overwhelmed with emotions, you can regulate yourself in a healthy way and overcome anything.

You don't have to figure it all out at once. Give yourself time to learn and grow with every up and down that is still to come. With a more positive mindset and a good idea of what positive coping skills look like, I know you can get through this and kick any negative coping habit you may have. Because that's what poor coping mechanisms are, simply bad habits used to cope with a difficult situation. You deserve better from yourself. Treat yourself with respect and embrace your differences to help you uncover the coping skills that you need to overcome depression and anxiety for good.

I know that overcoming bad coping habits and negative emotions is extremely difficult. But there is one more thing that can take your recovery and self-love to the next level. This final technique in Part 2 is all about learning to trust yourself after years of self-destructive behaviors and habits.

To help ensure that you are making good progress on your journey, chapter 8 will teach you how to use micro-goals to overcome or achieve anything in life.

8

MOVE YOUR MOUNTAINS WITH MICRO-GOALS

It is little keys that open up big doors.

– Lamine Pearlheart

With a deadline hanging over my head, dishes piling up in the sink, and the ever-present expectations of being a perfectly functional human being on my shoulders, I held the covers firmly over my head. Adjusting to adult life brought many challenges.

I was no longer a teenager who could get away with having a messy room, showing up late for class, or forgetting to brush my teeth. Adulthood meant being responsible, on time, and taking care of myself – things that seemed borderline impossible to maintain consistently in my mental state at the time.

Before my diagnosis, I held myself to an impossible standard of functioning for me. I beat myself up for every mistake I made and felt like a failure whenever I couldn't meet the expectations I was trying to live up to.

The expectations I am talking about came from the societal pressure that I felt, the pressure many of us feel in life. It's the pressure to succeed, to be healthy, good-looking, have a family, and become unrealistically happy all at once. This pressure, along with my own goals and desires, grew overwhelming very quickly.

On days like these, where having a deadline for a task was just the cherry on top of my overwhelm, the comforting thought of staying in bed was the only thing able to curb the feeling. I lay there, thoughts spiraling and body motionless. This is a perfect example of experiencing executive dysfunction without knowing it.

Before I explain what executive dysfunction is, I'd like to make it clear that I have by no means cured this part of being autistic. It will forever be a part of my life. This chapter is not about curing this problem because, for some of us, it can never go away entirely. However, I want to show you how I have been able to work around it, learning to live my life in a way that works best for me instead of trying to live in a way that society deems best.

Even as a happily diagnosed autistic adult, I still have to work hard and stay self-aware to keep up with normal day-to-day tasks like eating, housework, and managing my time properly. I still have days, now and then, where I feel glued under the covers. But this chapter is about how I get through executive dysfunction as best as I can and how you can too. I want to show you that it's okay to have down days and that there are ways to overcome them quickly without falling behind. You can stay on top of things and keep a forward momentum in your life by conquering executive dysfunction.

EXECUTIVE DYSFUNCTION AND SELF-ESTEEM

Executive dysfunction is the struggle to maintain good executive functioning. This is an extract from the American Academy of Neurology[5], "Executive functions represent a constellation of cognitive abilities that drive goal-oriented behavior and are critical to the ability to adapt to an ever-changing world." In other words, it's our brain's ability to motivate us to get tasks done in real-time. Life is not inactive; it is in a constant state of motion, even if we are lying under the covers in bed. Good executive functioning recognizes and accepts the ever-changing world, helping us to cope and keep up with it.

When you struggle to maintain good executive functioning, you will struggle with things like time management, working memory, inhibition, adjusting to change, and organization. This can look like:

- Repeatedly walking into a room and forgetting what you needed
- Struggling to be on time for engagements on a regular basis
- Being unable to exhibit good self-control either physically or vocally (echolalia)
- Feeling overwhelmed by a sudden change of plans or an unexpected life event
- Finding it extremely difficult to keep up with basic household tasks or hygiene

Executive dysfunction is a very common problem for people struggling with a variety of health issues and disorders including depression, anxiety, Autism, and ADHD. It is part of the reason why getting out of bed and following through with basic tasks can feel so impossible sometimes for so many of us.

Without understanding why you aren't able to keep up with certain things in life, it is only natural to assume that you just aren't trying hard enough or that there is something you are doing wrong. Soon the build-up of "failures" and "mistakes" kills your self-esteem. The more you decide that you're going to achieve something and fail due to an unrealistic approach, the more you lose trust in yourself and your abilities.

Luckily, this day in my life was not my first executive dysfunction rodeo, and I knew exactly what I needed to do to get myself out of bed and continue with my day. Being autistic, knowingly or not, feels like constantly having to negotiate and compromise with yourself in order to function and be happy. So that is what I learned to do.

I'm going to share the secret sauce that helped me cope with the executive dysfunction that was ruining my adult life. It helped me build trust in myself again, even before my diagnosis. And it helped me build my self-confidence to the point of knowing that whenever life gets overwhelming, I can keep going and do the things I set out to do.

This secret sauce was and still is, breaking overwhelming tasks into micro-goals and then acknowledging what I achieved in the day instead of thinking about what I didn't. This might seem simple, but when you are caught up in the crippling feeling of being completely overwhelmed, it helps to have an active strategy that you can use to dig yourself out of this powerlessness. So let's start with what micro-goals are.

THE POWER OF MICRO-GOALS

Traditional goal-setting can be a wonderful tool for most people to help them stay focused on what it is they want to achieve in life. While this is a great tool to have, it should not be the first line of action for making solid progress for everyone. Setting goals can become overwhelming and trigger shame or guilt when you don't achieve the goal. Can you see how this wonderful tool can backfire if you are struggling with mental health or executive dysfunction?

That is why the secret sauce to achieving the progress you truly need is by using a goal-setting technique called micro-goal setting, along with actively celebrating your achievements. Let's face it, some people's micro-achievements are other people's macro-achievements. You deserve to celebrate your wins, no matter how small they are in comparison to someone else's.

Micro-goal setting is the act of breaking down a regular goal or task into tiny bite-sized goals that are much more achievable. This can build your self-confidence and trust as you consistently prove that you do what you say you're going to do. Instead of focusing on a goal that feels like a tsunami wave raised up in front of you, you can focus on tackling the breakers instead. Very soon, this leads to an ocean of progress. The technique works for any goal but is especially beneficial for working around executive dysfunction.

For example, when I couldn't get myself out of bed to face the overwhelming amount of tasks and chores I had to do, including meeting a big deadline and doing the dishes, I broke everything down into much smaller goals, aka micro-goals. The first micro-goal was simply getting up. I acknowledged that getting out of bed was, for me, accomplishing a goal. I then approached every task that was looming in my mind the same way.

The giant pile of dishes was broken down into a list of categories that looked something like this: 1. Plates, 2. Bowls, 3. Cutlery, 4. Pots. I spread each category out across the day ahead and tackled them one at a time. For my executive dysfunction, doing them all at once, and without a clear structure, felt like too much and crippled me at the thought of it. But breaking the task down into stages allowed me to push myself in a healthy way and feel more capable of achieving what I set out to do. By the end of the day, the pile of dishes was gone.

For the next most daunting task, meeting my deadline, I set a time for myself to have the task done and broke down the work into increments. Thinking about working for 4 hours straight was crippling, but tackling the task 15-30 minutes at a time made the task feel more doable. I pushed myself to do 15-30 minutes, then rewarded myself with a quick break doing something I enjoy. Before I knew it, the task was done, and I was able to meet my deadline despite starting the day feeling like there was no way I could do it.

These are just two examples of how I managed to turn an overwhelming day into a personal success. Not only does breaking each task down into stages make the goals seem more attainable, but as each one gets done, the greater goal becomes smaller and more bearable. For example, once I had finished washing the plates, the pile of dishes became smaller and overall less intimidating.

The beauty of micro-goals for the struggling mind is that by the end of the day, instead of struggling to complete two big tasks and feeling like a failure, you complete several smaller tasks, rewarding yourself along the way while ultimately completing the two bigger tasks as well. Even if you don't manage to complete the bigger tasks completely, you are still able to appreciate and celebrate what you DID do rather than beat yourself up for what you didn't.

You can break down tasks into as small of a goal as reasonably necessary to help override the executive dysfunction. For example, if you need to write an essay but it feels impossible because your executive dysfunction is robbing you of all motivation to do it, start by writing the first sentence.

Instead of thinking about finishing the whole essay, if you stay focused on simply writing one sentence at a time, you will have accomplished a goal, and your self-esteem will be intact. Don't worry about how long it takes you; just try to stay focused on the task. Once you reach this micro-goal, remember to give yourself a small reward like a short break, a cup of tea, or just a smile and a kind thought about your progress. This way, instead of feeling like you didn't get the essay done, you can look back on your day and see that you are one step closer to reaching the complete essay.

This comes back to the importance of a good mindset in the pursuit of happiness and self-love. If you are constantly focusing on what you didn't get done instead of being proud of what you *did*, despite all your challenges, you are never going to feel like you're succeeding in life.

Most people don't complete every task they set out to do each day. So if you have a tendency to beat yourself up or feel like a failure as I did, then micro-goals can help you better quantify all the effort you ARE putting in rather than holding yourself to an unrealistic expectation.

CELEBRATE YOUR WINS

Micro-goals are not going to be effective if the voice inside your head is still spewing negativity at you. I can't stress enough how much you need to pay attention to how you talk to yourself. With the help of chapters 6 and 7, I trust that you are already making progress in this regard. If not, go back and review these chapters and review your Workbook. This book is dense with information, and I advise you to keep it handy in case old patterns emerge, and for most of us, they usually do. It can mean the difference between long-term recovery and constantly relapsing depression. Your Workbook is filled with positive work you've accomplished, and spending time reviewing and revising will ensure you stay on track toward your self-love and acceptance. Remember, you're not going to stay happy if you're constantly talking down to yourself.

This is why celebrating your wins every time you reach a micro-goal is so important. Learning to celebrate your small successes can give your inner voice a positive boost. Setting yourself micro-goals and acknowledging every achievement will help to improve your self-confidence and self-esteem, allowing you to view yourself in a more positive light. You can change your internal narrative from "Why can't I just grow up and do it?" to "Wow, I did it even though it felt impossible!"

You have to realize that everyone has different levels of day-to-day functioning and capabilities. You can still do the things you set your mind to, but you might have to adjust your expectations regarding how quickly you reach your goal. You might also have to adjust your approach so that you can reach your goal in a way that is more realistic to you and your executive functioning.

Imagine a giraffe, a rhino, and an eagle cross a wetland. Each animal has different strengths and weaknesses to get them to the other side. One has long legs for covering distance, one has wings to fly over it, and one has more strength to push through the reeds.

Each animal will get to the other side at their own speed and will have to approach the wetland in a way that works best for them. You can't expect a giraffe to fly over the wetland, you can't expect an eagle to push through the reeds, and you can't expect a rhino to cover the distance as quickly as the others. None of the three animals are failures for achieving the same goal in a different way.

In the same way, you are not a failure for getting what you need done in your unique way. If you are struggling with executive dysfunction because of Autism, depression, ADHD, or anxiety, you can't expect to do things the same way as someone else. Even if we don't suffer from any of these conditions, we all have different strengths and weaknesses, so play on your strengths, accept your weaknesses, and understand that it's okay to reach your goals in a slower or more unconventional way.

Don't be afraid to break up any task that feels overwhelming to you into as many stages as you need to. I know that when you are struggling with severe depression or having an experience like a panic attack or meltdown, even the simplest thing, like remembering to breathe or forcing yourself out of bed, can feel impossible. I want you to remember the concept of micro-goals in these times as well, never forgetting to celebrate your smallest wins.

The more you focus on the progress you are making, the more likely you are to keep on moving forward and do your best every day. With micro-goals, you have proven to yourself that you are capable of doing what you set your mind towards. Very soon, you will realize that you are not, by any means, a failure. Your confidence will soar to the point that you believe in yourself more than you ever have before.

Your self-confidence and trust in yourself are vital to continue making progress along your journey toward lasting happiness and self-love. When things get tough, and you feel like life is impossible again, you will have built up enough strength and trust in yourself to KNOW that you can pick yourself up again and make it through the dark just like you have before.

Along with your mindset shift and unique toolbox of coping skills at your disposal, you have built yourself a solid foundation to stand on. Now, I'm proud to say that you are ready to move on to Part 3 of this book and learn what you can continue doing forever to make sure that the incredible progress you make along your journey lasts.

PART 3

What To Do Forever

9

THE TRUTH ABOUT THERAPY

Just because no one else can heal or do your inner work for you doesn't mean you can, should, or need to do it alone.

– Lisa Olivera

My heart pounded as I arrived at the gate of my first appointment with Joan. My dad had given me her number after I decided to see a therapist a few weeks following my hospitalization. Her gate was overgrown with roses that had crept up the bars, blooming into a beautiful display of blush pink and twisted green vines. With a deep trembling breath in, I took a step forward and pushed the buzzer.

Prince, the stallion, was already in my life, but I had not started riding horses yet. I was still caught in the throes of agoraphobia, daily panic attacks, and severe depression. The thought of leaving the house for this appointment terrified me, but I had to choose love if I wanted to survive this. Fear wasn't going to get me anywhere good.

The gate lock released, and the tall wooden front door of Joan's house opened gently. I walked down the brick steps, past her gate, and arrived at the door. With a warm smile and an encouraging swing of her arm, she welcomed me inside.

Before this day, I had only seen one psychologist and an unlicensed psychiatrist. Both of whom I believe only did my journey harm. I had seen my first psychologist for a few sessions after I had started self-harming at 13 but left every session feeling broken down. The unlicensed psychiatrist I had seen at 16 was, in my opinion, trigger-happy with his diagnoses and drug prescriptions. He never gave me any direction on what to do about my illness besides popping a handful of pills. In comparison to Joan, these two were chalk, while Joan was cheese.

After my experience with Joan, therapy became one of my most valued tools for recovery. On its own, it would not have sufficed.

But paired with the methods I have shared with you in Parts 1 and 2 of this book, it helped me stay focused on the way forward when my mind felt too chaotic to remember what to do next. Each session would help give me the clarity I needed to make my own decisions in resolving my problems. And if something from the past would come up, she would help guide my thought process to shift those emotions for myself.

Speaking to Joan was not the same as getting advice from a friend or loved one. It was a safe space for me to go where I knew I could verbalize my deepest fears and concerns and have them land on non-judgemental ears every time. It was a place where I could speak my mind and reflect on the things coming up for me, both in my current life and deep into the past.

However, if my mindset were not open to hearing Joan's feedback or following through with my own revelations that came during a session, nothing in my life would have changed. I had to make the best of the guidance she offered and use my sessions to the fullest by being as open and as vulnerable as possible.

I want to make something very clear here; therapy is not a cure for mental illness. Therapy is merely a tool to help cushion the fall and support you while YOU pick yourself back up again. A therapist does not give you all the answers or figure anything out for you. They are a sounding board to help guide you back on track when your life becomes derailed by a sudden change or resurfaced trauma. You have to be willing to approach each session with vulnerability and allow the therapist to work with you to guide you through the process of figuring out what to do for yourself. You have all the answers within you, but a therapist can help unlock them faster and more productively than you might do yourself during a low point in your life.

I'm not saying it isn't possible to recover without therapy, but seeing a therapist or engaging in some form of therapy that works for you, can speed up your recovery significantly. Sometimes mental illness can also progress to the point where your ability to think clearly and make good choices for yourself is severely compromised. This is where therapy has a solid role in a recovery journey and should not be dismissed out of fear or prejudice.

When it comes to deciding whether or not you would like to try therapy, there are two things you need to consider. Firstly, you need to ask yourself whether you urgently need therapy, and secondly, what type of therapy you're willing to try.

If you are unsure whether or not you are comfortable trying therapy, please know that it is completely warranted to seek professional help of some kind, no matter how severe or mild your symptoms may be. Therapists are only there to support you, and everyone can benefit from active support in their lives.

THE DIFFERENT FACES OF GOOD THERAPY

Throughout my journey, I have inadvertently partaken in a wide range of what I would consider therapy. Although I did pay to see a qualified psychologist and have since seen a qualified psychiatric specialist to receive my Autism diagnosis, I still attribute a very large portion of my recovery to my involvement with horses.

My time with horses has never been under any therapeutic context, but horses themselves are known to be very healing animals to spend time around. I'm telling you this because Equine-assisted therapy is a valid form of receiving support, and there are many other alternative ways to get therapy without sitting down in a clinician's office.

While I do vouch for finding a psychologist that works for you, as well as seeking an accurate diagnosis for your struggles, if needed, I also want you to know that everyone is different. The type of therapy that works for me might not work for you. This is why I want you to be open to seeking a form of therapy that does.

However, before you can seek the type of therapy that feels right to you, it helps to understand the role those different therapists can play along a mental health journey. You might end up working with your own personal "team" of therapists to assist your progress. For me, it was regular appointments with Joan, occasional visits with my psychiatrist up until my diagnosis, and daily sessions training and working with horses.

It helps to understand the difference between the various types of mental health professionals and know that there are options beyond them as well.

TYPES OF THERAPY AND WHAT THEY ARE GOOD FOR

Psychiatry: A psychiatrist is a mental health professional specializing in the diagnosis and medical treatment of mental illness or disorder. They are the only type of mental health professional able to prescribe medication or diagnose.

Psychology: A psychologist is a mental health professional who studies the mind and behavior. Their role in a recovery journey is to help people learn to cope and adapt to new ways of thinking by listening and helping to identify thoughts and behaviors that could benefit from redirection. They are also able to refer you to a psychiatrist if they feel a diagnosis would benefit you.

Counseling: A counselor is a mental health professional trained to help people identify solutions to mental health problems, build better communication and coping skills, encourage positive mental shifts, and counsel people through difficult situations.

Life Coaching: A life coach is a wellness professional trained to help people make positive shifts and progress in their lives in order to reach better happiness and fulfillment. These sessions are often less about figuring out the past and more about creating a brighter future.

Alternative Therapies: There are a wide variety of properly recognized and reputable alternative therapies available, including equine-assisted therapy, art therapy, movement therapy, meditation coaching, aromatherapy, hypnotherapy, psychedelic-assisted therapy, and more.

While there are many forms of therapy you could try, it is very important that you start somewhere you feel most drawn to and comfortable with. Working through mental struggle is never comfortable, but it is important that you have a good mindset and outlook for the therapy that you choose. However, above all, always keep in mind that no therapy can work for you on its own. Only you can take what you've learned during a session and apply it to your life for a positive outcome.

It is also important to note that different types of therapy work best for different degrees of mental struggle. Understanding where you are on your recovery journey will help you determine which type of therapy is the best start for you or whether you need therapy at all.

DO YOU NEED THERAPY?

Since going through years of drowning in my struggles, feeling failed by the professional help I initially received as I desperately yearned for the right support, I had never given therapy the acknowledgment it deserves. Now, looking back on the years of good therapy that came later, I can see the incredible role it played in my long-term recovery.

Just as an example, without Joan, I don't believe I would have had the courage to leave my failing marriage feeling confident enough in my own thinking to trust my instincts. She gave me a space to talk openly about how I felt and helped me decipher which thoughts and feelings were normal for a healthy relationship and which ones were serious red flags. If I did not have her support, I can almost guarantee that I would have stayed in a marriage where I felt trapped, scared, and isolated. It was a marriage that did not have the room I needed to heal.

In my case, I needed an experienced psychologist and eventually a psychiatrist to see my mental transformation through. Getting my diagnosis has been one of the most life-changing things to ever happen to me and has given me vital insight into who I am to help me live my life, love myself, and be happy in a way that works for me and my neurotype. My only regret is not meeting Joan sooner or learning that I was autistic before I tried committing suicide.

However, if you can learn anything from my experience with therapy, don't wait. If you are struggling to the point of feeling like you can't carry on moving forward anymore, seek professional help. Your health and safety is the most important thing along your healing journey. Without you, there is no journey left to go on, and that's what life is all about. You are here to experience life with all its complexities. As much as there is hardship in the world, there is so much good! Don't let one bad decision take that opportunity away from you.

Remember, nothing lasts forever. Life is in a constant state of flux, and our attitude toward life has a tremendous impact on whether we believe it is working for or against us. Life is filled with moments, good, bad, and neutral, and our response to these moments can influence how we will feel in an hour's time, a day's time, a year's time, or even 10 years' time. So instead of suffering in silence if you go through a rough patch, there's nothing wrong with reaching out for help.

If at any point you feel that you are not able to keep moving forward on your own, professional help should be your first line of action in order to make sure that you can progress safely. Just because you have everything you need within yourself doesn't mean you don't need help unlocking that knowledge from time to time.

A counselor or psychologist is always a great place to start, as they will quickly be able to determine whether or not you need to be referred to someone more experienced than them. On the other hand, after a few sessions, you might have received the support you needed and feel like you can carry on without therapy for a while or try a less intensive form of therapy. There are no rules to what does or doesn't work for your personal healing journey. Everyone is unique, so gauge what feels right to you.

I always say,

 "Everyone can benefit from therapy,"

and what I mean by that is that there is a form of therapy out there for everyone that will improve their life. Even if you are doing fairly well mentally, why not squeeze every drop out of this existence and continue deepening your healing journey? We can never fully know and understand everything there is to know in this one lifetime. There will always be days when attending an art therapy class, speaking to someone knowledgeable, or trying something new will uplift you. That's what therapy is! Or at least that's what therapy can be.

TIPS FOR A GREAT EXPERIENCE

As you can see from my journey, the biggest setback therapy caused me was continuing to see mental health professionals that were not working well for me. To make sure your experience is great from the word go, here are some things I recommend giving some thought to before throwing in the towel after one bad experience:

Choose the right therapist: Finding the right therapist can be like trying on shoes, not every pair is going to fit you. But once you find the style you like and know your size, it can fit like a glove. Make sure you choose a form of therapy you feel comfortable with and give one appointment a go. If you don't enjoy the experience, you can always try another therapist or therapy form.

Pay attention to how you feel: During a therapy session, pay attention to the way that it transforms your feeling and behavior. If you were jittery before, you might still be jittery during the session or even feel worse, but how you feel afterward is what's important. Sometimes it takes a couple of sessions before you feel the peace that a good therapy session can bring, but trust your gut instincts and keep track of how the therapy is working for you. Use your Workbook to track your research on therapies and therapists. Then you can also use your Workbook to track your experiences and progress.

Be open to hearing uncomfortable things: A good therapist might pick up on certain behaviors or thought patterns you are showing. If your therapist does make you aware of something negative in your behavior, it can be uncomfortable. But it is important to stay open to hearing the difficult things in order to see the most growth.

Be prepared to be vulnerable: Even if it takes you a few sessions to get completely comfortable opening up, being as vulnerable as you can be with a therapist you trust can help you get the most out of every session.

Stick with it: As we've established, recovery is a journey. You can't expect one therapy session to completely change your life. Therapy is a process that can take time to fully reap all the benefits. Be patient, and try to stick with it if you're not seeing signs of progress.

When considering whether or not therapy is something you want to try, or continue on with, consider your unique needs and trust your instincts. You don't have to see a therapist for anyone else but yourself. In the same breath, you shouldn't hold yourself back from receiving the support you might need because of a prejudice against therapy.

Release any shame or guilt associated with getting help. Even if you end up having a trusted therapist by your side for years to come, because life will always have its ups and downs, understand that it is merely another tool to help you cope and overcome the struggles you may face.

Humans are not on earth to live life in isolation. We are social beings that need each other to thrive. So, with a good therapist by your side, you can use their support to continue lifting yourself up and doing the work to become the best version of yourself. From the minute you leave the appointment to the minute you step into that next session, that is where your opportunity to make progress lies. The work that you do will make all the difference.

Remember, it doesn't matter how much therapy you do or don't get. The journey to feeling better starts from within. Nobody will ever know you better than you can know yourself, so complete the activities in your Workbook then turn the page to chapter 10, and I'll tell you what the final, most important step is to achieve lifelong progress towards loving yourself and feeling better than ever before.

10

TRUST THE PROCESS, YOU'RE A WORK IN PROGRESS

There is no standard normal.
Normal is subjective. There are seven billion
versions of normal on this planet.

– Matt Haig

Feeling the thuds of my fist vibrate through my body as I lost control, I sat helpless on the floor. Like a computer stuck on "the blue screen of death," my brain became stuck in a short circuit of overwhelm. With the intense urge to hit my own head with my fists, I punched my arms and legs instead to divert the energy somewhere less destructive. I grasped onto any slither of restraint I could muster and desperately waited for the meltdown to be over.

In a few moments, exhaustion took over my body, and the usual surge of guilt, shame, and sorrow ensued. Being an adult makes it difficult to accept that meltdowns and shutdowns are, more often than not, a part of the autistic deal. However, no matter how much I am aware of that, it doesn't make having them any easier.

I often feel obligated to be put together, well-balanced, and on top of things all of the time. But being autistic means having struggles that are mostly out of my control. For example: When the sound of the neighbor's dog barking feels like a jackhammer on my eardrum. When the subtle fold of my bedspread creases against my skin, nagging me to move "just one more time," leaving me sleepless for hours. When a small argument becomes blown out of proportion because of my mismatched tone of voice and body language. Or when a friend suddenly cancels a plan without enough warning to mentally prepare myself. Meltdowns can hit out of the blue.

While knowing what my triggers are helps me to negate a meltdown at the best of times, sometimes I simply can't avoid it. Accepting this part of my life, in all its potential ugliness, is still something I am working through. It is also something very uncomfortable for me to share with you.

However, it is important I share this final detail of my life to show you that progress is not always pretty. Yours will never look the same as someone else's, and it is often not what you expect. I want you to understand that you, along with every other human on this planet, are a work in progress. You will never be a perfect version of yourself. Perfect doesn't exist. Moments of ugliness are part of the human experience.

Recovery from depression and anxiety, or any other mental struggle, will never be one-size-fits-all, nor will it ever happen overnight. Your journey is going to be completely unique, and making sure to treat it as such is what will help keep your expectations more realistic. You can't look at someone else's journey and expect things to go the same way for you. Plus, we never get the full picture of someone else's journey. Our interpretation of others is subjective and should not be used to belittle or limit ourselves.

Your journey is your journey. If you can respect that, trusting that the effort you put in will have a positive effect, then you will see progress. Even if that progress is not always pretty, any progress is good progress.

EMBRACING THE FULL SPECTRUM OF EMOTIONS

You are going to experience the full range of human emotions over the course of your life. Even when you do all the *right* things to keep yourself happy and stable, life has a way of throwing curveballs. I'm not saying this to scare you or take away your hope for better times, but it is important you become comfortable with this. You need to be prepared for the emotions you may have to work through.

Emotions are not inherently good or bad. Yes, some don't feel very comfortable, but each one has a purpose. Each emotion has a time and a place where it is necessary to feel a certain way. You need to release any judgment towards yourself and your emotions in order to move through them when they come up. Being prepared for them helps.

Trying to avoid emotions, or ruminating on them, can keep you stuck in an emotional state where you attach too much meaning to the emotion. This gives emotions power and makes processing them a lot more difficult.

When you can release judgment towards an emotion and simply respect how you feel, you can work through the "bad" emotions much faster. The sooner you can process "negative" emotions, the sooner you can get through a bad patch and keep moving forward.

This takes practice and consistency, but you will get better at it with time using the techniques you've learned in Part 2 of this book. The better you can get at staying above your emotions, allowing them to flow through you, rather than getting stuck in them, or bottling them away, the better you will get at picking yourself back up again when you fall. This is what this chapter is all about.

You need to embrace the full spectrum of human emotions and give yourself leeway to have ups and downs without judgment. As long as you are consistently trying your best and moving forward as best as you can, give yourself credit.

THE KEY TO LONG-TERM HAPPINESS

Just like a slowly dripping tap can overflow a sink, the small steps you take to keep moving forward and making progress, no matter how messy or slow it is, will inevitably build up to big results.

The key to maintaining your happiness and self-love for the long term is never giving up. Your consistency in sticking to the things that work for you, and pushing through even when you feel like you've lost hope, is how you can stay above bad times no matter what.

No matter how many times you fall down, getting back up again is the essence of a successful recovery. If you are determined to rise above your struggles each and every time, nothing will ever be able to beat you down - at least not for very long.

Life's ups and downs are inevitable for everyone, so don't shy away from that fact. Instead, understand that even if you are doing well right now, there may come a time when you feel like everything comes crashing down on you. Quit ruminating on what might or might not happen, and put your focus on building self-love and trust within yourself to become unbreakable.

You have learned skills that allow you to bring light into a dark moment, use them and watch your confidence grow. Go to your Workbook now and complete the exercises waiting for you, then continue on right here when you're done.

If bad times happen, and you trust yourself to get through them, nothing will be able to stand in your way. You won't worry about the outcome; you will simply KNOW that you're going to be okay again. This knowing and trust come from your determination, time, and work put in towards building that for yourself. The more trust and self-love you have, the harder giving up becomes.

However, sometimes in the swing of chaos, we slip down a dark spiral, and it happens nonetheless. We fall down and feel like square one has become too familiar for our liking. But remember, when you are in a dark place, you don't have to stay there.

YOUR JOURNEY IS COMPLETELY UNIQUE

Leading up to my Autism diagnosis; meltdowns had become an uncomfortably regular occurrence. Although I was solidly on my recovery journey, which meant that I had already stopped self-harming for quite some time, I was still having meltdowns. I had started to meditate regularly, exercise, and eat healthily. I was largely happy in my new relationship, lifestyle, and life path. But a monumental piece of information was missing from the picture.

The pressure to balance everything was exhausting with all the added stressors of adulthood, from making money, paying bills, driving a car, and keeping up a romantic relationship to maintaining friendships. My battery was perpetually empty, and I had little energy left to cope when things went wrong. The minute something bad happened, I would panic and fixate on the negative things happening in my life. Meditation helped, but the benefits only lasted until the next bad thing happened.

Although I had started seeing Joan again during this time, it soon became apparent to me that there might be something more going on other than just depression or anxiety. The more I would speak to Joan, or search the internet, hoping to find out what was happening to me during these moments of extreme overwhelm, the more confusing everything became. Then I stumbled upon a video of someone talking about meltdowns and other things related to Autism.

Immediately dismissing the thought that I could be autistic, I did nothing for quite some time. But after a couple of months, things had not gotten better, and I booked an appointment with the closest psychiatric specialist. There was no way I could continue experiencing these meltdowns with no credible explanation as to what they were or why they were happening.

Without that explanation, it simply seemed like I was throwing a really bad "tantrum." You can see how that would pose a problem in my home life. I struggled to receive the support or empathy during these times of extreme stress, which further aggravated and intensified the experience. It wasn't a problem I could ignore without risking permanent damage to my relationships.

Since my diagnosis, I have been able to adjust and accept many aspects of my life. I can also see where I was going wrong and why my battery was always empty. Now that I am learning to understand myself on a new level, I have been able to recover and live in a way that fits me and my neurotype. I have seen lasting progress and have been coping with bad times better than I have ever been able to before.

This is where understanding yourself and tailoring your recovery and life around your needs comes at a serious advantage. Sometimes you can be doing "everything right" from the standpoint of what works for most people but forgetting to factor in your own differences and abilities. You have to remember that your journey is completely unique and keep that in mind when things go wrong.

I also want you to know that my life has not been void of difficulty since my diagnosis, either. I have found myself overwhelmed, down, and ready to give up many times, including more recently. However, my ability to consciously redirect the thoughts and emotions that took me to those places of despair has become a superpower.

I am able to fall down, reaching depths I hadn't reached in years, and pull myself out unscathed, ready to keep moving forward. This is the final thing you need to know in order to do the same for yourself. You need to know the one thing you have to do if you spiral down that dark hole of depression or anxiety again in the future. Keep reading!

WHAT TO DO IF YOU SPIRAL AGAIN

Unfortunately, something that happens all too often when we fall into a dark place is that our minds seem to go through a sort of sweep. We forget all the things that help us cope in a positive way, and forget what worked for us before. Our minds also like to play along with whatever thought spirals are going on, and reaching out for help often seems impossible.

When you fall down and reach depths that you hoped you would never have to visit again or even depths beyond those, there is one thing you have to do: Remember! The only thing you have to do in those darkest times is remember what worked for you before and how you have overcome bad times in the past. Yes, you can learn new things, but in the depths of despair, simply remember the techniques you've learned throughout this book:

- Mindfulness
- Journaling
- Practicing gratitude
- Viewing things more objectively
- Setting and celebrating micro-goals
- Exercising positive coping skills
- Reaching out for help
- And more!

The power of these tools should not be underestimated. They were critical in my healing

You have so many tools at your disposal; you simply need to remember them when things go wrong.

Even if those bad times do not compare to the present moment, what worked for you once, is very likely to work for you again. So if, for whatever reason, you find yourself at square one, I challenge you to pick up this book, pick up your Workbook, and start from the beginning. Ask yourself, "Am I okay?" and go through each chapter once again. Let this book be your resource.

Although you are starting from square one, you are not starting from scratch. Every time you fall down, you pick yourself back up with the strength and tools you have gained. Know that every time you feel like you are slipping, you are a different version of yourself than the time before. Remember that you are stronger, more knowledgeable, and have more trust in yourself. You will overcome each downfall better than the last if you simply *remember* how far you've come and who you are now.

Think of it like muscle memory. Each time you break down and rebuild yourself, you will retain what you have learned from that experience. You will have a better understanding of who you are and what works for you; all you need is reminding, and it will all come back to you in due course.

Eventually, your trust and understanding in *you* will be so solid that you won't even question whether or not you will make it this time. Since reaching this point in my life where I can comfortably release the labels of depression and anxiety from my identity, I no longer hold onto the fear of coping with difficulties in the future. I know that hard times will come again, but I no longer have to feel anxious about whether or not I will make it through. The trust I have in myself and the self-love I have built carry me safely to shore from the stormy oceans of life's peaks and falls.

With the tools I have built up along my journey, the same ones I have shared with you throughout this book, I KNOW that I will make it through hard times like I have done every time before. When hardships sail up over the horizon of my life, I embrace the journey and emotions that come with them. I take the time

I need to process the difficult emotions and remind myself of all the things that help me stay afloat as the tides come and go.

Just like me, with time, you will simply KNOW that you can, and you will get through hard times again. You will reach the shoreline and remember how to breathe when you're drowning. Remind yourself of all the things you need to do to make it happen. And if you forget, this book will be here waiting for you.

You have all the tools. You have the strength and knowledge within yourself to never give up and keep moving forward no matter what. Staying consistent with the things that are working to improve your life and remembering what those things are when you fall off the bandwagon is going to allow you to confidently trust that you've got your recovery in the bag.

I can't begin to explain how happy I am to share this journey with you, so let me give it a try as we conclude this part of your journey together. I am very proud to say that you have made it to the end of this final chapter and can now turn the page so that I can see you off on the best note.

Thank you so much for allowing me to share my story with you. I hope I get to meet you one day and hear yours.

IN 90 SECONDS YOU CAN MAKE A HUGE DIFFERENCE

If you feel we've deserved it, please take a moment to leave a review on Amazon.

Your feedback means the world to us. It helps us to improve and it means better learning experiences for all our readers.

We'd be so grateful to you for your review!

CONCLUSION

Along with all the invaluable stories, messages, and lessons I have left you in this book, the number one thing I need you to embrace is this: Only YOU can change your life.

This book is not about saving you, it never was, and it never will be. Instead, this book is a tool for you to carry and hold with you along your unique journey. It will always be here to refer back to when you've forgotten how to switch on the light of healing for yourself.

You've got all the strength and knowledge within you to live a life of self-love, abundant joy, and true happiness. Once you've learned and understood that you have had the power to overcome the darkness all along, you will conquer any obstacle the future may hold.

But this revelation does not come without self-awareness, self-work, and a persistent will to keep on fighting no matter how many times you fail. You have to be willing to do the work, stay consistent, and give it everything you've got.

I've never once doubted your willingness to help yourself. If you weren't willing, you wouldn't have made it to the end of this book, or you might not have picked it up at all.

I know that you've got the willpower to go far. I know that you are fully capable of tackling your journey with determination. So prove it to yourself, and take what you've learned here into your everyday life. Let it become your reference whenever you feel like things are crumbling. Let it remind you that loving yourself and being happy IS possible. You don't have to stay strong on your own either. Stay in touch on the LearnWell Community.

NOW KEEP GOING

Keep making progress and keep fighting until you leave the tunnel behind you. You've worked so hard to transform the lens you view life through. You have to keep it polished.

You've got the tools at your disposal, and you know how to pick yourself up. So do it even if it takes time. Even if it takes effort or you get knocked down again. Just keep going and trust that it will be worth it.

I want you to look back on your life one day and thank yourself for all the steps you took when you felt like you couldn't carry on anymore. I need you to keep making progress, no matter how ugly or slow it may be at times. Embrace yourself in all your authentic beauty and see that you are worth so much more than what you've been through.

Allow this new version of yourself to emerge from the cocoon of mental struggles you've been wrapped in. Stay mindful of yourself and the way you interact with life, continuing to shift and retrain yourself to live a life of love.

Soon enough, you will find yourself soaring to heights you never thought you'd reach. And even then, keep going. Learning to fly is boundless.

REFERENCES

1. The serotonin theory of depression: a systematic umbrella review of the evidence, Joanna Moncrieff https://www.nature.com/articles/s41380-022-01661-0

2. From Neurons To Neighborhoods: The Science Of Early Childhood Development, https://www.ncbi.nlm.nih.gov/books/NBK225550/

3. PubMed Central: Mindfulness practice leads to increases in regional brain gray matter density https://www.ncbi.nlm.nih.gov/pmc/articles/PMC3004979/

4. The Substance Abuse and Mental Health Services Administration (SAMHSA): CHILDREN LIVING WITH PARENTS WHO HAVE A SUBSTANCE USE DISORDER https://www.samhsa.gov/data/sites/default/files/report_3223/ShortReport-3223.html

5. PubMed Central, American Academy Of Neurology: Executive Dysfunction https://www.ncbi.nlm.nih.gov/pmc/articles/PMC4455841/

www.ingramcontent.com/pod-product-compliance
Lightning Source LLC
Chambersburg PA
CBHW020416080526
44584CB00014B/1354